RIVERSONG OF THE RHONE

(CHANT DE NOTRE RHÔNE)

RIVERSONG OF THE RHONE
(CHANT DE NOTRE RHÔNE)

By Charles Ferdinand Ramuz

Translated by Patti M Marxsen

ONESUCH PRESS

LONDON   MELBOURNE   NEW YORK

Onesuch Press enriches lives by reclaiming the forgotten past; publishing the lesser known works of great writers and the great works of forgotten ones. For more information visit www.onesuchpress.com

A Onesuch Bilingual Edition
Published by Onesuch Press
PO Box 303BK, Black Hill 3350 Australia

Translation © Patti M. Marxsen, 2015
© Onesuch Press, 2015

National Library of Australia Cataloguing-in-Publication entry
Author: Ramuz, C. F. (Charles Ferdinand), 1878 — 1947, author
Title: Riversong of the Rhône : Chant de notre Rhône
by Charles Ferdinand Ramuz
translated by Patti M. Marxsen
foreword by Susan Tiberghien

ISBN: 978-0-98-740143-4 *(paperback)*
ISBN: 978-0-98-740144-1 *(ebook)*

Subjects: Prose poems, French.
Rhône (France)
Other Authors / Contributors:
Marxsen, Patti M. translator
Tiberghien, Susan, foreword

Dewey Number: 841.912

The paper used in this publication meets the minimum requirements of ANSI/NISO Z39.48-1992 (R1997) (Permanence of Paper). The paper used in this book is from responsibly managed forests. Printed in the United States of America, the United Kingdom and Australia by Lightning Source, Inc.

FOREWORD

Riversong of the Rhone is a beautiful book. And still more beautiful if we take the time to listen to it as well as to read it. To listen to the song of the river. It is the music that turns the pages, that tunes the heart of the reader to the beauty of the words. To the beauty of the Rhone River and its riversides, the home of the author—and composer—C.F. Ramuz.

On my first reading of Patti Marxsen's superb translation of Ramuz's *Riversong*, I was carried along with the river, flowing from high in the mountains of Switzerland, through the little lake, a cradle with the French province of Savoy on one side and the Jura Mountain range on the other, all the way down to the big lake, the Mediterranean. Marxsen knows well the movement and the sound of the Rhone River, as she too has made her home in the country of Ramuz. I was listening to a fugue, a musical composition of many voices, each voice harmonizing with the others, a whole, a riversong. My mind wandered from the riverbanks to the vineyards, to stand alongside the *vignerons*, as they harvest the grapes and "gather themselves in the wine that contains them, contains their life, and them, and the best of their acts, at the same time that it contains the sun and the soil from whence it came."

On my second and slower reading—slower because of my deepening appreciation of each line as translated by Marxsen—I was reminded of Charles Baudelaire who wrote almost a century earlier, "Who among us has not dreamed of the miracle of a poetic prose … supple enough and jarring enough to be adapted to the soul's lyrical movements?" Ramuz has given voice to Baudelaire's dream of a poetic prose.

If we look at the opening lines, we find all the elements of fine poetry: "They are picking grapes in the vineyards above me, suspended above me among stone walls, suspended half-way up the steps with baskets called *hottes* on their backs. When full, the weight is great, they bend beneath this weight, suspended beneath it from the full height of the sky, they are suspended on the mountains...

There is repetition: "suspended...suspended...suspended" creating a spell. There is rhythm: the iambic beat of "when full, the weight is great..." a short syllable followed by a long, creating a rhythmic melody. There are word sounds: the repeated sound of the "s," and rhyme: the internal rhyme of "great ... weight ..." that makes us listen to the scene. And there are images: the *vignerons* are visible, suspended, yet bending down under the *hottes*, the baskets of full of grapes. All we would need to write *Riversong* as a poem would be line breaks. Instead, in writing it as prose, Ramuz lets the lines meander, supple and jarring, as the river meanders through "days of blue water, days of green water, days when the wind turns the water completely black."

In this way *Riversong* adapts itself to the soul's lyrical movements. We become mesmerized by the rhythmic song of the river. We let ourselves drift through the world that Ramuz has created. That he has painted, for just as we listen to *Riversong*, we see *Riversong*, "I paint it again, one more time saying: Look, the shape of its riverbanks is like a cradle; its interior takes the form that it pleases." And slowly we ourselves become part of the river, "wild, savage, or so caressing, which depends on the day and the weather, so blue, so sparkling, and other times the color of slate, like blossoming clover, like a young girl's check, like the faces of old men, stitched and restitched with wrinkles, the color of earth." A cascade of similes, like the cascade of water, so blue, so sparkling. We see it almost palpably, soft like a young girl's cheek, unruly like the wrinkles in the faces of old men.

The translator, Patti Marxsen, has made this possible. For close to a century *Riversong* has remained unknown to English language readers and C.F. Ramuz, one of Switzerland's greatest writers of

the twentieth century, has remained underappreciated. I digress here a moment to speak of translation, of its importance and of its art. How many writers have not been brought to our attention because they have not been translated? How many works have not been appreciated, have not been given life because they have not been translated? Translation is more vital than ever today in our multi-cultural world. If we cannot read the voices of the unknown, the unrecognized, how can we pretend to be multi-cultural? Translators are the ferry men and women of the world's literature.

Ramuz's writing is immensely difficult to translate. If we read the Translator's Note, we get a glimpse into the many faceted conundrums of translating C.F. Ramuz. Marxsen has taken French lyrical prose and transformed it into English lyrical prose. I would say "magically" transformed, yet it is not through magic that she has done this—although there is also a bit of magic in her work—but through the art and craft of translation. Not only has she found the right words and the right language, but she has also discovered the pitch, the chords, the silences to make *Riversong* sing. Marxsen has been able to do this because she is both translator and prose poet herself.

I have read with growing admiration most of Patti Marxsen's work from her ekphrasic poems like "Girl Braiding Her Hair," which was published in the journal *Ekphrasis*, and "Madame de Staël," which appeared in *Offshoots12: Writing from Geneva*. I am also familiar with her imaginative stories in *Tales from the Heart of Haiti* that capture the mystery and beauty of Haiti and her *Island Journeys*, a collection of skillfully wrought essays of travel and place. She follows in in the footsteps of C.F. Ramuz, and of Baudelaire, writing a poetic prose that reflects the soul's lyricism.

Herein lies the secret of the brilliance of *Riversong of the Rhone*. The author/poet C.F. Ramuz and the translator/poet Patti M. Marxsen have come together as a pair of alchemists, like in the Middle Ages when it was most often a pair, heating the alchemical furnace, stoking the fire, to burn away the impurities and find the gold in the base metals. Together Ramuz and Marxsen have listened to—looked at—the river, there "where it begins to glisten white and you see it flee toward the west." They have distilled the gold and shared it with us in *Riversong of the Rhone*.

Susan M. Tiberghien
Geneva-based author of
Looking for Gold;
Circling to the Center;
One Year to a Writing Life;
Footsteps;
Side by Side, Writing Your Love Story.

On Translating Ramuz's Riversong

Creating an English title for C. F. Ramuz's epic prose poem has been my first and last challenge, as it was for the poet himself. His journals tell us that as late as October 1919, his working title was *Berceau du Rhône-Cradle of the Rhone*, though by the time he sent the manuscript off to his Geneva publisher in mid-November, it carried the title *Chant de notre Rhône*. I began with a literal translation of that: *Song of Our Rhone*. Then, as I read the French aloud to myself, I felt pulled toward the melodic *Riversong of Our Rhone* with its extra syllables and repetitive "R." These features announce Ramuz's fluid, musical text in which the river itself "sings" through the voice of the poet. For above all, this text is an ode of epic dimensions with a poet at the center who "sings" his hymn to the Rhone as if it were a lover or a God. There is an echo of a classical chorus in his recurring refrains, a pleasing rhythm that resonates through the themes of this work: a universal human connection to nature, spiritual ancestry embodied in place, the power of progress, the yearning and necessity for love in all its forms. In an effort to encompass this wide scope, I eventually altered Ramuz's regionally possessive "notre" ("our") to the more universal definite article, a simple "the." And with this universality in mind—often sheathed in classical overtones that convey a sense of grandeur—I have retained the archaic "ô" throughout the poem. Ramuz uses this one-letter word often to signal a sense of awe. The more colloquial English "Oh" would have sounded more like a sigh.

But for all of Ramuz's universal reach and classical sensibility, *Riversong of the Rhone* is also quite modern. There is no mythological quest here, no wandering to conquer foreign worlds, no Oedipal conflict or moral dilemma to resolve. There is, rather, a singular, subjective narrator reflecting on his place in the wake of World War I. The poet seems to speak from a riverbank or a hillside overlooking Lake Leman, considering the blessed corner of the world that exists, thanks to all who have come before him and loved it

as he does. Some aspects of the poem and its tone will feel familiar to American readers of Henry David Thoreau, who exalted the simplicity of nature from the woods near Walden Pond, or of Walt Whitman. Like Ramuz, Whitman asserted his uniqueness even as he linked himself to the vast collective spirit of America in poems like the 1892 version of "Song of Myself," where the poet's view of the world is "sung" in the opening lines: "I celebrate myself, and sing myself, / And what I assume you shall assume, / For every atom belonging to me as good belongs to you."

Ramuz, writing decades later, makes a similar claim in similarly musical language when he writes of those who harvest the grapes as they "… gather themselves in the wine that contains them, contains their life, and them, and the best of their acts, at the same time that it contains the sun and the soil from whence it came." He "sings" of these people and their deep connection to the land that relies on the Rhone, proclaiming "…all of us as a unity and of who we are, the proclamation of kinship … in the sense that we are a region of the world, and a part of the world, being the ones that we are who hold together thanks to a similar way of loving."

Mindful of the "grandeur" Ramuz wishes to express in his "music," I have tried to strike a balance between my obligation to his text and the translator's task of recreating the text through the prism of another mode of expression. Compromises have, inevitably, been made. Throughout this poem, freely associated thoughts and powerful images cascade forward, often separated by a succession of commas and semi-colons, as a choral music composer might indicate breath marks. Some paragraphs—if pages of uninterrupted text can be called paragraphs—break infrequently. Elsewhere, single sentences stand as a succession of "paragraphs," even when the thread of thought could be gathered into something resembling a block. I have, for the most part, left this "architecture" as I

found it, even if the ultimate goal of translating "feeling and meaning" cannot be achieved through mirror-effects of punctuation and paragraph breaks.

The greater challenge relates to untranslatable vocabulary, the thick layer of cultural translation, and the matter of word choice to achieve an equivalent effect. In a work like this, there are points when a word carries more weight in French than English. In such situations the translator must ask: When is it right to retain the original French? This translator's response: When the word embellishes meaning and also remains understood, perhaps with a few cultural cues. A simple example is the phrase "*langue d'oc*," which I have defined the first time it is used as a "language from this south." Ramuz does not define it at all because his readers would not have required an explanation. It should be also noted that when Ramuz writes, "*... la langue qui parlent les hommes*," I have removed the "sexism" that would exist in a literal translation of that construction— "... the language spoken by men,"—because it is clear to me that he is referring to the language spoken in the region, by all people who live there. This oblique "gender issue" arises more than once, not because C. F Ramuz was a misogynist, but because he was writing in an era when the use of "his," "he," or "mankind" was assumed to encompass to both genders. Where possible, I have tried to "erase" confusion where it appears through the magic of language. That said, there is no doubt that gathering in the wine cellar to decant an aged bottle of wine was a strictly masculine ritual, just as the *vigneron* himself, the wine maker, is male.

More complicated yet is the vocabulary of Swiss viticulture. This presents a number of challenges to the translator who wishes to use the original language sparingly. Consider the *hotte*, an enormous wood-framed basket made to be strapped to the strong backs of grape pickers. *Hotte* is an untranslatable word, not least

because it is a rare sight in our world today. (Metal containers are more common now.) "Basket"—even "wooden basket"—is inadequate because it suggests a container too light-weight to hold 80 pounds of grapes, as did the sturdy *hotte*. Nor do American-style "baskets" typically attach to the backs of human beings. Quite apart from these practical matters, the word "*hotte*" gives us an authentic sound—like overhearing a moment at the cracked door of the past—that adds to the world portrayed. *Pressoir* does the same thing, but *pressoir* also touches on problems of non-equivalence, for the enormity of the heavy, wooden contraptions that pressed grapes a century ago can hardly be conveyed with the whispering sound of "wine press." Having decided to use these words in the original language, I proceeded to retain *vendange* and *vigneron*. Of course, I could have used "grape harvest" and "wine maker," but the mood of authenticity in French had already been established and had to be maintained. Such decisions inevitably relate to the translator's assumptions; in this case, that such words—as well as the name of the wine region east of Lausanne *(Lavaux)* and the various grapes cultivated there *(muscat, fendant, humagne, rèze, amigne, dézelay)*—fall within the "cultural curiosity register" of the potential audience for this work.

This text was first published in 1920 by a man of classical tastes who had studied and loved the literature of Antiquity. Thus, while the use of "whence" or "from whence" will sound outdated to modern ears, such expressions convey a timeless quality that is entirely appropriate to Ramuz's voice. I also pondered the distinction between "look" and "watch," since Ramuz's *regarder* can mean either. My frequent preference for "watch" relates to the nuance of anticipation it conveys. Likewise, Ramuz's *"dire"* does not always work poetically if translated as "I say" or "I am saying." From time to time, I stretched the nuances a bit toward statements such as "I

speak" or "I announce," and freely used the commonplace present participle in English (the "–ing" form) that is implied by the present tense in French because, for all his "classicism," Ramuz also believed in the poetic power of ordinary speech.

With spoken language in mind, I chose "grind and crack" for *grincer* and *craquer* to preserve the resonant consonants, since this option was available to me, even though *grincer* can also mean: squeeze, creak, grate, or gnash (as with teeth) and *craquer* can even be made to "squeak," a word far too small for the deep meaning represented by the wine press, the mighty *pressoir*. In an effort to keep the slurred sound Ramuz tried to emulate when he wrote *"ces minuit"*—where he dropped both the apostrophe and the "t" of *"c'est minuit"*—I brought this into English as "s'midnight." And since Ramuz plays with spoken language when he writes *"mon cric-crac à moi"* to convey the clattering sound of the *pressoir's* gears, I preserved his onomatopoeic word choice with "click-clack rhythm." It goes without saying that another translator might have chosen other solutions and justifications for all of these words and phrases.

It is likely, however, that all translators would agree on the importance of repetition in Ramuz's Riversong. This literary device serves a variety of functions from emulating spoken language to setting the tempo of the poem to creating an "audio image" of the over-arching metaphor: the ever-flowing river. The chanting, incantatory spirit of the Rhone is, in fact, the essential "song" of this text:

> I see the water, I find the water, I find the Rhone and the lake; I find the spaces of the lake to be the father of all the rest, because this lake was born elsewhere and this lake carries itself elsewhere, because this lake is a river, because this lake has a course of its own to follow.

This passage represents a classic Ramuzien digression into repetition. If compromises are made—as I made when I added "of its

own to follow" at the end of the last line—they must be justifiable in terms of rhythm and flow. If a literal translation of repetitious lines causes the poem to slow down and stumble, then the repetition must be "massaged" and paced to achieve its aim in English. In this text, Ramuz's "music" always matters more than a word-for-word translation because his rhythm and flow are deeply entwined with meaning.

A final challenge confronted by each and every English translator of Ramuz is what we might call the "pronoun problem." It is simple enough in English to assert distinctions among our pronouns: one, you (singular), you (plural), we, and they. But writing becomes complicated when these clearly definable words collapse into Ramuz's multiple vantage points that, furthermore, extend to the generalized inner self of the poet. Ramuz includes this inner self in his "we" and "you," just as many English speakers imply its existence when "one" is used as a subject. A phrase like "One does not speak of certain things in public" includes the speaker, after all. But a too-frequent use of "one" sounds unnecessarily formal for the rustic/classical register of *Chant de notre Rhône*. In the end, if Ramuz refuses consistency by mixing his vantage points and, therefore, his pronouns, I decided that the translator might also consider herself liberated from "good grammar" and do the same.

Taking Ramuz's approach to heart as a kind of permission, I often changed the third person pronoun "one" to "you." Instead of sticking close to his "... *savoir qui on est, savoir d'où on vient, savoir où on va*,"—which would sound like this in English: "... to know who one is, to know where one comes from, to know where one is going,"—I opted for "to know who you are, to know where you come from, to know where you are going." In my view, this resists the distant formality associated with "one" as the tone shifts to a perspective that is both more direct and more interior for English

language readers. In other attempts to avoid the formality of "one," I have used the impersonal "we" or "they" that English freely allows.

One could certainly argue that no permission has been granted, that all pronouns should be replicated, come what may. By way of self-defense, I have respected Ramuz's choice whenever possible, especially when he deliberately chooses *"vous"* to shift the point of view in order to speak directly to his readers and / or pull them in with a jolt of immediacy. In my view, Ramuz's *"vous"* should most often be read as a plural to suggest "all of you." Quite apart from the collective scope of his work, I am quite sure that Ramuz had the confidence to imagine more than one reader taking an interest in his work. (Note that he addresses the Rhone as *"tu"* and *"toi,"* both more intimate and familiar than the polite distance of a singular *"vous."*)

In Ramuz, that sometimes startling "you" often serves as a kind of pivot that allows the point of view to shift quickly and easily, as if the poet suddenly realizes that YOU are listening. At one point in *Riversong*, the narrator speaks of the girl who "saves herself by making fun of you." Then the voice speaks to that girl, admiring her "copper combs that you made yourself." Such twists and turns echo—consciously, I would argue—the winding course of the river as Ramuz blends the unpredictable movement of the Rhone with the equally unpredictable energy of time and change, of youth and young love that mingles with the imagery of dark glossy hair as full as "a bunch of grapes." The river, like the girl's hair that is evoked a second time at the end of the poem, becomes a symbol of time itself.

The over-arching theme of *Chant de notre Rhône* is the unstoppable flow of time. To imagine time itself reflected in the river as it travels through Switzerland and France is a way of making visible

the immeasurable grandeur of nature that has determined the lives of those who were born along these shores. Those who have lived and worked here together, shared the secret hidden in the wine, loved each other, prayed together, and died beneath the same sky. In *Riversong of the Rhone*, the poet's soul observes all of this and more, then sings it onto the page. "Others might sing of an empty soul: one sings here of the soul of a river, and this soul never dies."

Patti M. Marxsen

Acknowledgments

This translation exists because C.F. Ramuz's grandson, Guido Olivieri, kindly replied to a letter I wrote in 2008, thereby granting permission to proceed with a translation. He was acting on behalf of his mother, Marianne Olivieri-Ramuz who watched over her father's publications for more than half a century. Both of these people—who devoted many years to honoring the work of their famous relative—have now passed on. It is, therefore, to the Estate of C.F. Ramuz that I express my gratitude for permission to bring this epic prose poem into English for the first time. Like the Rhone itself, the best literature flows through time and speaks to one generation after another.

I also wish to thank Susan M. Tiberghien for adding the contribution of an insightful foreword to her busy schedule of writing and teaching. If I have become a sort of prose poet in my own right, it is thanks, in part, to her workshops of the Geneva Writers Group that she founded over twenty years ago.

Finally, my husband, Hans-Peter Müller, deserves my ongoing gratitude for his support of my work. I have only come to know Switzerland because of Hans-Peter and he is, among other things, a connoisseur of the fine Swiss wine that forms a central metaphor in "*l'espace ramuzien.*" As the poet says at the end of his *Riversong*, "nothing is born without love."

Patti M. Marxsen
Thun, Switzerland

BIOGRAPHIES

Charles Ferdinand Ramuz (1878-1947) was a native of French-speaking Switzerland who became a prolific and important novelist, as well as a beloved poet-of-the-people. His first works were collections of poetry published during early in his decade spent in Paris (1904-1914). He went to Paris in search of his artistic voice after earning a *licence ès lettres* in classical literature at the University of Lausanne. In time, he would return to Switzerland, teach, write, and collaborate with Igor Stravinksy on the still-popular *Histoire du Soldat (A Soldier's Tale)* that was first performed in Lausanne in the final months of World War I. Ramuz also authored twenty-two novels, several of which were made into films in his lifetime, as well as an epic prose poem, *Chant de Notre Rhône*, first published in 1920.

Charles Ferdinand Ramuz, named for the child who preceded him in his parents' home but did not survive, lived most of his life in Pully, a village on the shores of Lake Leman. In 2005, definitive versions of his novels appeared in the prestigious, leather-bound Pléiade Edition of the Parisian publisher Gallimard. *The Complete Works of C. F. Ramuz*—including his journals, early writings, theatrical pieces, and poems—have been published in multiple volumes by Éditions Slatkine of Geneva. A photographic portrait of Ramuz appears on the Swiss 200 franc note that travels through Switzerland every day. In more ways than one, he remains close to the people he honored with his work.

Patti M. Marxsen's articles, essays, poetry, and reviews have appeared in over 40 publications in the USA, Switzerland, and France, including *Caribbean Writer, Ekphrasis, Fourth Genre, The International Herald Tribune, Journal of Haitian Studies, Offshoots: Writing from Geneva, Prairie Schooner, Saisons d'Alsace, Women's Review of Books*, and *The Writer*. Among her writings, Marxsen has been active in the field of Haitian Studies and also authored two articles on C.F. Ramuz in *The French Review* (2008) and *Absinthe: New European Writing* (2009). Her books include a collection of travel essays—*Island Journeys: Exploring the Legacy of France* (Alondra Press, 2008), which was a finalist for the Non-Fiction Book Award of the Writers League of Texas. She has also published a collection of short fiction—*Tales from the Heart of Haiti*, which was a finalist for the 2008 Paris Prize for Fiction before it was published by Educa Vision Inc. of Miami, Florida (2010).

Marxsen's work in Schweitzer Studies has also been noteworthy. Her translation from the French of *Albert Schweitzer's Lambarene: A Legacy of Humanity for Our World Today* by Jo and Walter Munz appeared in 2010. More recently, her carefully-researched biography of Albert Schweitzer's wife, *Helene Schweitzer: A Life of Her Own*, was published by Syracuse University Press in Spring 2015.

She has twice been nominated for a Pushcart Prize and achieved a Special Mention in the 2009 Pushcart Anthology with her travel essay, *Alone in Amsterdam*. Another travel essay, *Gâteau de Payerne*, won the Geneva Writers Literary Award for Non-Fiction in 2013. Patti Marxsen lives in Switzerland and travels frequently to Maine.

Riversong of the Rhone

(Chant de notre Rhône)

The original edition of Chant de Notre Rhone by C. F. Ramuz on which the present translation is based was published in Geneva by Georg & Company Publishers in 1920 with a frontispiece woodcut by Henry Bischoff

Dans les vignes au-dessus de moi ils sont occupés à cueillir; ils pendent au-dessus de moi parmi les murs, ils pendent à mi-hauteur des escaliers avec leurs *hottes*.

Quand elles sont pleines, le poids est grand; ils penchent sous ce poids et pendent sous ce poids en pleine hauteur du ciel, le mont debout dedans; et eux pendus au mont, et moi au-dessous d'eux.

Sur cette rive qui est la mienne, je me suis mis tout contre l'eau.

Je me tiens tout à fait au pied du mont, là où la petite vague vient en rampant comme le chat, et la grande se lève en l'air sur ses pieds de derrière comme le cheval qui se cabre.

Heures du temps, heures marquées, une grande horloge est là, qui bat.

Miroir de la vie et du ciel, un grand miroir est là où je me mire.

Et le mont aussi qui s'y mire, et moi, mis à côté, tâche de saisir cette double image, l'utilisant ensuite comme le lac lui-même fait par l'expression de sa voix, les phrases dites, les mots prononcés; qui bat le temps, qui marque l'heure; qui règle le ciel, qui décide de l'air; maître à chanter et maître à dire, et en tout genre de choses dites.

They are picking grapes in the vineyards above me; suspended above me among stone walls, suspended half-way up the steps with baskets called *hottes* on their backs.

When full, the weight is great; they bend beneath this weight, suspended beneath it from the full height of the sky; they are suspended on the mountains that stand up straight within the sky, and I am down here below them.

On this shore that is my own I set myself completely against the current.

I stand firm at the foot of the mountain, there where the little wave comes crawling like a cat, and the big one pulls back in the air like a horse rearing up on its hind legs.

Hours of time, marking time on the great clock that is always there, ticking.

Mirror of life and sky, a great mirror is there in which I am reflected.

And the mountain, too, is reflected there and me, stepping aside, I try to seize this double image, using it like the lake itself that speaks phrases, pronounces words that express its own voice; the lake that keeps time, measures the hour; that determines the wind; master of songs and master of the spoken word, and of all things that can be named.

Une grandeur s'exprime devant moi: si seulement je pouvais l'exprimer. Aujourd'hui qu'on fait la vendange et tout le mont bouge de gens occupés à cueillir, à entasser, et à fouler, c'est-à-dire récolter, c'est-à-dire se payer de leur travail et de leurs peines, c'est-à-dire se résumer dans le vin qui les contient, contient leur vie, et eux, et le meilleur de leurs actions, en même temps qu'il contient le soleil et le sol d'où il est sorti, — s'il y avait pourtant un autre vin, né aussi de ce pays, né d'un homme de ce pays, et qui le contiendrait et contiendrait le pays.

Midi vient, je regarde, la journée s'avance.

Quelles richesses, je me dis, autres que d'abord ce poisson pris aux mailles chaque jour devant chez moi par les hommes dans un bateau vert sous une voile, mais autres encore que ce poisson.

Cueilli abondamment, pièce à pièce, aux mailles, jeté dans le fond du bateau brillant et ruisselant comme de la monnaie neuve, mais l'autre poisson, celui des images, celui des idées, celui des mots, tout remuants aussi de vie; quelle richesse de pêcheur d'idées et de vigneron de grappes de mots, oh! encore due quand même à ce lieu, qui m'a été choisi comme le mien.

Travailler en plaisir, comme on dit en musique, et comme ils font ou vont faire dans les pressoirs, en musique: la musique des pressoirs.

Quand la vendange grince et craque, coulant à petit fil et puis à gouttes dans la tine, les hommes se tenant assis sur un

A grandeur expresses itself before me: if only I could express it. Today is the day of the wine harvest, the *vendange*, and the entire mountain is in motion with people who are here to pack in the grapes and pile them up, which is to say to harvest these grapes, which is to say to gather themselves in the wine that contains them, contains their life, and them, and the best of their acts, at the same time that it contains the sun and the soil from whence it came,—if there were, nevertheless, another wine also born of this land, born of a man of this land, that too would contain him and would contain the land.

Noon is coming, I watch as the day advances.

What riches before me, I say to myself, apart from, first of all, the fish taken in with nets in front of my home by men in a green boat under sail, other riches still than these fish.

Gathered abundantly, piece by piece, in the nets, tossed on the boat bottom as shiny and slippery as newly-minted coins, but the other fish, that of images, that of ideas, of words, all quivering, too, with life; what riches are collected by the fisherman of ideas and the *vignerons* with their clusters of grapes and words, the *vignerons*, oh! the riches, nevertheless, of this place that has been chosen as my own.

To work for pleasure, as one says in music, as they do or will do in the pressing of wine, as in music: in the music of the *pressoirs*.

When the harvest grinds and cracks, running in a little trickle and then in drops into the vat, men holding on, seated

banc pendant ce temps: ces minuit, deux heures du matin; est-
ce qu'on va refaire une pressurée, ou redonner un tour? Mais
rien ne presse, et en attendant ils mangent un morceau.

Une chandelle est dans le chandelier de fer forgé, la main qui
porte le morceau à la bouche est au plafond une grosse main
noire; pêcheurs, *vignerons*, pressureurs; cueilleurs de poisson,
récolteurs de grappes, encaveurs de jus; et moi cueilleur de
quoi jusqu'ici? récolteur de quoi jusqu'ici? quand même tant
d'autres choses sont à cueillir et d'abord ce ciel même, cette
eau, ses rives; cueillir d'où cette eau vient et où cette eau s'en
va.

Mais travailleur parmi les travailleurs, mon cric-crac à moi,
qui est de la pièce d'acier tombant à chaque dent dans l'en-
tre-deux des dents pour empêcher que ça n'aille en arrière; ah!
que pour moi non plus, ça n'aille pas en arrière, quand l'amas
du foulé durcit, se dessèche par excès de pression, ne laisse déjà
plus tomber qu'un peu de suc, mais le meilleur.

Ah! être associé, à tout ce qui est d'ici, mais en vue d'une
nourriture dépassant ici, comme il arrive quand la nourrit-
ure est bonne, c'est-à-dire qu'elle l'est pour tous les hommes,
comme l'est le poisson quand il est bon, comme l'est le vin
quand il est bon.

Midi, je regarde, la journée s'avance.

L'heure est venue qu'il faut maintenant connaître la courbe
de l'astre (et en général toute courbe); et, ayant connu d'où
l'astre sort et par quel chemin il est venu jusqu'ici, connaître
également quel chemin il va suivre jusqu'à l'endroit de son
coucher.

on a bench all the while: s'midnight, two o'clock in the morning; is someone going to give it another press, another turn? But nothing is pressing here as they have a bite to eat while waiting.

A candle is in the cast iron chandelier, turning the hand that brings food to mouth into a large black shadow overhead; fishermen, *vignerons*, pressers; gatherers of fish, harvesters of grapes, keepers of juice in the wine cellars; and me, a gatherer of what up until now? Harvester of what until now? Anyway, there are so many other things to be gathered, first and foremost the sky itself, this water, these shores; to gather from the source of this water and the place to where this water is flowing.

But worker among the workers in my own click-clack rhythm, that sound of steel teeth falling together so not to slide back; ah! that I, too, may not slide back and fall behind when the mass of crushed grapes hardens and dries under excessive pressure, letting nothing else fall but a bit of juice, the best.

Ah! To be connected to all that is here, but in view of nourishment that goes beyond this place, as happens when nourishment is good, which is to say for everyone, like the fish when it is good, like the wine when it is good.

Noon. I watch as the day advances.

The hour has come when it is necessary to know about the curving arc of the sun (and, in general, about all curvatures); and having understood where the sun rises and how it came to be here, to know as well which path it will follow to find the place where it sets.

Connaître, savoir, déduire; rapprocher selon les similitudes et les parentés; mettre ensemble ce qui va ensemble; se mettre d'abord à sa place; savoir qui on est, savoir d'où on vient, savoir où on va; chanter ensemble une origine, le point atteint, le point à atteindre; le berceau, le cours, l'élargissement, l'embouchure; la petite leçon que c'est, puis un peu plus, puis toujours plus; le retentissement dernier parmi toute la mer.

To be familiar with all this, to know, to deduce; to bring things together according to resemblance and kinship; to put together what goes together; to put oneself, first of all, in one's place, to know who you are, to know where you come from, to know where you are going; to sing of one origin together; of the point we have reached, of the point waiting to be reached; the cradle and the movement that rushes forward, the expansion, the opening; the small lesson here is that there is always a little more, then still more; until we reach the last reverberation of the entire sea.

L à-bas, né du glacier: et voilà d'abord l'origine.

C'est cette grande vallée pierreuse, avec un versant privé de sa chair sous une peau peinte et repeinte, cuite et recuite par le soleil, où si souvent on s'est tenu, à l'ombre de l'un ou l'autre de ces pins qu'il y a, l'ombrelle des branches mal ouverte et un peu de travers, en peinture vert foncé sur une peinture bleu foncé; et on l'a contemplé de là, dans le fond de cette vallée, quand il coulait encore blanc comme sont les eaux du glacier qui sont des eaux comme du lait.

Sur ce fond plat était la route, sur ce fond plat était la véritable route, sur ce fond plat était la voie ferrée; sur ce fond plat était cette autre fausse route, plus large, plus tortueuse, avec ses volontés, beaucoup plus large, avec ses fantaisies, prenant en travers tout à coup, puis faisant un contour, puis de nouveau tout contre la montagne, comme si elle cherchait l'ombre, puis de nouveau droit devant soi.

Les villages étaient posés à plat tout auprès de rochers pointus.

Des épines de rocs perçaient partout cette croûte de sable.

Une ville vient, deux grandes épines de roc sont à côté; déjà elles portaient, déjà elles avaient chacune sa couronne de pierres bâties, l'une le château fort du seigneur, l'autre la maison de Dieu.

Et voilà, dès ici, partout autour de moi et en dessous de moi les vignes; ils labourent dedans pour les irrigations et creusent des fossés où ils couchent les ceps afin de rajeunir la sève, tra-

There, born of the glacier: and there it is, the original source.

This great stony valley, with a private sloughing off of flesh beneath a skin that has been painted and repainted, baked and rebaked in the sun, where we so often stand riveted in the shade of some pine tree or other, in the shadow of barely opened, criss-crossed branches, a brushwork of dark green against a canvas of dark blue; and one has thought about the river from there, in the depth of this valley, when it still flowed white as glacial waters are, waters the color of milk.

The route was on this flat bed of land, on this flatness was the true way through, on this flatness was the railroad track; on this flatbed was the other false route, larger, more torturous, with its own will, greater still, with its fantasies, changing direction all of a sudden, then twisting and turning, then again going against the mountain as if searching for shade, then right there before you.

The villages were placed on the flat bed of land, right next to rocky outcroppings.

Everywhere, spikes of rock pierced this crust of sand.

A city comes, two great jagged rocks next to it; already they carry something, already each one has its crown of beaten stone, one the strong castle of a nobleman, the other the house of God.

And there it is, from here all around me and below me the vineyards; the vines laboring within for irrigation and carving ditches where the stocks are resting in order to rejuvenate in

vaillant avec peine contre la perte d'ardoises culbutées, et ces carrés de vigne également sont culbutés.

Ils tombent, ces carrés, les uns par-dessus les autres, penchant dans des sens différents, des petits hommes noirs dedans, avec une langue qu'on ne comprend pas, bien qu'elle soit la nôtre, —moi plus haut sous les pins et tout près le rocher commence, la nudité des lieux où trop de soleil donne et un peu de terre était et a été emportée, alors il ne reste que les ossements.

Quand les carillons me venaient, ces soirs et ces matins et ces midis de cloches, ces dimanches tout du long, ces fêtes; le pays entier pour des fêtes et des dimanches se mettant à parler en cloches, et elles aussi parlaient et parlent la *langue d'oc*, qui est la langue que parlent les hommes; premier patois de *langue d'oc*, à ta source même, dès ta source, ô Rhône.

Pour quoi d'abord tu es ici, mais tu es ici pour beaucoup de choses.

J'écris ici d'abord le lieu de ta naissance, cherchant à le marquer aux yeux; c'est ce pays pierreux et tout peint d'un côté, quand l'autre projette son ombre.

Églises, vieilles et neuves, petites et grandes, églises de pierre, la pierre partout, la vigne partout, ici déjà les étages de vignes, les vieilles vignes, les vieux plans, muscat, fendant, umagne, rèze, amigne, l'une sur l'autre par étages et marches du côté du nord (là le roc, là la nudité): dès le début de toi, s'affirme une nature, laquelle se retrouve dans les mots dits, les gestes faits, la couleur de la peau des femmes, leurs tresses tellement serrées qu'elles font penser à une grappe de raisins.

their sap, working hard against the erosion of tumbling slate, and the plots of vines are tumbling too.

They fall, these terraces, one after another, leaning in different directions, small dark shadows of men with a language no one understands, even though it is our own,—from higher up beneath the pines and very near to me the rocks begin, I see the nakedness of places where too much sun pours from the sky, where there was only a little earth and the earth has been carried away, until nothing remains but bones.

When the carillons reached me, these evenings and mornings and noontime church bells, these long Sundays, these holidays; the entire countryside is beginning to speak in church bells of its celebrations and of Sundays, and they, too, were speaking and are speaking the language of the south, the *langue d'oc*, the language spoken here; the first dialect of the *langue d'oc*, right at its source, your source, ô Rhone.

To begin with, why are you here? But you are here for many reasons.

I write above all of your birthplace, searching to mark it with my eyes; it is this stony land, all painted on one side while the other projects its shadow.

Churches, old and new, small and large, stone churches, stone everywhere, vineyards everywhere, here already these terraced vineyards, the old vines, the old plots of *muscat, fendant, humagne, rèze, amigne*, one on top of another planted on terraces and steps along the north side (there, the rock, there the nakedness): from your first appearance here, nature affirms itself, an affirmation found in spoken words, in acts, in the color of women's skin, their long hair braided so that it reminds you of a bunch of grapes.

13

Premier cours, et droit devant toi.

Un peigne de cuivre est dedans. Elles ont les pieds tout petits.

Mains pour des gros ouvrages et durs, et des gros souliers à ces petits pieds et le caraco gris sans forme qui tombe tout autour de ce qu'il entend cacher, et quand même: parce qu'il cache trop; — baisse la tête, est-ce pour pouvoir mieux rire, est-ce parce que tu es honteuse? elle met la tête dans ses mains et puis tout à coup se détourne, et puis se sauve en se moquant de vous, ô toi qui avais les cheveux comme une grappe de raisins noirs et, ces peignes de cuivre, tu te les fabriquais toi-même; — les jours de messe, les dimanches à orguettes, les danses défendues dans les fenils là-haut; — souvenirs, premier cours, là-bas quand le Rhône commence, pays vécu, pays gouté par moi dans toutes ses productions (des amignes vous bougeant au bout des doigts, c'est des vins nerveux comme ils disent, des vins de goût aussi et des vins de couleurs, des fendants en lambeaux de couleurs devant vous); — souvenirs, premier cours du Rhône, et droit devant lui, tout d'abord; puis tout à coup il tourne à angle droit entre deux rochers, là où saint Maurice, le 22 septembre 286, est mort pour sa foi avec les dix mille Martyrs de la Légion thébaine; et dès ce temps une basilique a été là, qui y est encore, qu'on va voir, qu'on va visiter, et son trésor byzantin, égyptiaque, syrien, toutes les très vielles reliques, les bouteilles de vrai sang cachetées avec de la cire qui date du temps des Romains, ce chef d'argent, avec une fenêtre pour laisser voir le crane, qui fait penser à une tête

The first flow of the river, right before your eyes.

Copper combs inside their hair. They have very small feet.

Hands made for hard, heavy work, large shoes on their small feet and the formless gray camisole that falls all around the hidden things understood to be concealed, but come now: it conceals too much; — does a lowered head allow you to laugh more easily, because you are ashamed? she puts her head in her hands and suddenly turns, and then saves herself by making fun of you, ô you who had hair like a bunch of black grapes, and these copper combs that you made yourself; — the days at mass, the Sundays of playing the harmonica, the forbidden dances in the haylofts up there; — memories, the first ripples of a riverway where the Rhone begins in the lived-in land, the land tasted by me in all its bounty (the *amignes* that make your fingers tingle, one of the "nervous wines," as they say, the best wines too and the colorful wines, the *fendants* in striated color there before you); — memories, the first rush of the Rhone, and right before you, before everything; then suddenly it turns at a right angle between two rocks, there where Saint Maurice died on September 22, 286, died for his faith with the ten thousand martyrs of Rome's Thebaine Legion; and since that time a basilica has been there that is still there, that people go to see, to visit with its Byzantine, Egyptian, and Syrian treasures, all the ancient relics, the bottles of true blood hidden by wax that dates back to Roman times, the shiny helmet with a window to let you see the skull of a chief

de momie, tellement tout est vieux ici, et pourtant tout est neuf, parce que tout est frais et pas encore dit, ô très vieux, très jeune pays, très vieux Rhône, toujours plus jeune.

that makes you think of the head of a mummy because everything here is so old, and at the same time everything is new, because everything is fresh and not yet said, ô very old, very young land, the ancient Rhone, always and forever younger than everything else.

Je regarde tout le temps le Rhône.

Ici à présent est le berceau: je regarde bouger le berceau, avec ses rives en bordure.

La savoyarde, la vaudoise.

Je regarde bouger le berceau entre les deux rives rejointes du bout qui donnent au berceau sa forme, et inégalement elles sont mises en vis-à-vis.

L'ouvrage n'est pas tellement égal qu'il ennuie, le bon ouvrier n'ennuie pas, le bon ouvrier ne fait pas trop égal, le bon ouvrier s'amuse à des différences.

La savoyarde, la vaudoise.

Tu ne peux pas te plaindre de l'Ouvrier, ni te plaindre de son ouvrage, n'est-ce pas? ô toi qui es là, et déjà tu remplis la couche que tes parents t'ont préparée, cette Savoie et ce Pays de Vaud, ici, maintenant que tu es couché, la Savoie à ta gauche, le Pays de Vaud à ta droite, celle-là poussant du pied le berceau qui penche vers nous, et nous du pied le repoussant, qui penche à nouveau de l'autre côté.

La Savoie à ta gauche, le Pays de Vaud à ta droite, tu as un temps à tes côtés, ici quelque chose comme tes parrain et marraine, et soucieux de toi ils te bercent en mesure quand, en effet, par les beaux jours, on voit cette surface s'incliner dans l'autre sens.

I watch the Rhone all the time.

At the moment, I see a cradle: I watch the cradle rocking, a riverbank on each side.

The side that is Savoy, the other that is the Vaud.

Here and now is the cradle: I watch the cradle move, with its border of riverbanks.

The Savoyard side and the Vaudois.

I watch the cradle rocking between the two riverbanks joined at the ends, giving the cradle its shape and, at the same time, placing them asymmetrically across from each other.

The shape of things is not so equal that it tires the eyes, the good laborer is not tiresome, the good laborer avoids a perfect shape, the laborer amuses himself with differences.

The side that belongs to Savoy, the other that is the Vaud.

You cannot complain to the Great Laborer, nor can you complain about his work, can you? ô you, who are the one who is there and already you fill the bed your parents have prepared for you, this Savoy and this Vaud, right here, now that you are resting, the Savoy on your left, the Vaud on your right, the latter pushing the cradle with its foot so that it leans toward us as we push it back with our feet, so that it leans anew to the other side.

Savoy on your left, the region of the Vaud on your right, you feel the rhythm on both sides here, like being surrounded by your godfathers and godmothers who, caring for you as they do, they are able to rock your cradle steadily so that, on those days when the weather is fine, you see this surface incline in one direction, then another.

Pays doux et grands, pays bien de toi, et dignes de toi.

Là-bas, sous la montagne, ils ont la châtaigne et les treilles; on les voit qui jouent aux boules devant des petits cafés. Ils ont des pantalons de velours, ils ont des ceintures rouges, ils portent des bérets de feutre. Ils ont des carrières de marbre noir qu'ils font sauter à la cheddite (alors vite ils vont se cacher, il n'y a plus rien, il y a un temps où tout est désert, où tout fait silence, c'est quand la mèche est en train de brûler); ils ont des bateaux de pêcheurs, ils ont des filets fins comme s'ils étaient faits avec des cheveux de femme, ils ont des grands filets moins fins; ils allument des lanternes à des bouées dessus; ils ont leurs grandes barques à pierres, ils ont leurs belles grandes barques noires à pierres et l'œil qui est devant, une fois qu'elles sont chargées, tout à coup se tourne vers nous sous les voiles qui retentissent, puis se gonflent en s'entrecroisant; la Savoie là-bas, leurs treilles, leurs carrières, leurs forêts de châtaigniers, leurs villages à noms de Saints: Saint-Gingolph, Meillerie, Évian, Saint-Paul, Thonon, Nernier, Yvoire; mais à présent faisons le tour, et c'est nos villages à nous, avec des noms de Saints aussi: Nyon, Rolle, Saint-Prex, Morges, Saint-Sulpice, Lausanne, Cully (ma ville) (et ici je me tiens, étant au centre pour mieux voir), Saint-Saphorin, Vevey, Clarens, Villeneuve.

Cette double rive par les bouts se joint, formant l'ovale du berceau, et c'est une seule rive.

Le parrain et la marraine aux deux bouts du berceau se tiennent par la main.

Sweet, great country, the country that is your own and worthy of you.

Over there, beneath the mountain, they have chestnut trees and grape arbors; you can see them playing boules in front of the small cafés. They wear corduroy pants with red belts and they wear berets of felted wool. They have black marble quarries there where they use cheddite explosives (then they duck quickly for there is nothing more after that, there is moment when it's all desert, all silence when the fuse is burning); they have fishing boats, and fine fishing nets, as if they were made out of women's hair, and they have bigger nets that are less fine; they light their buoy lanterns up above; they have their long stone barques, their big beautiful barques made of black stone and once the craft is loaded the eye out front turns toward us under its sails that pull back, then fills to criss-cross with the force of the wind; Savoy over there, their grape arbors and quarries, their chestnut forests, their villages named for saints: Saint-Gingolph, Meillerie, Evian, Saint-Paul, Thonon, Nernier, Yvoire; but first let's have the tour, and here are our villages named for saints too: Nyon, Rolle, Saint-Prex, Morges, Saint-Sulpice, Lausanne, Cully (my city) (and here I hold on, being at the center where I can see better), Saint-Saphorin, Vevey, Clarens, Villeneuve.

This double riverbank joined at its two ends forms the oval of a cradle, and so it is one riverbank.

The godfather and the godmother at each end of the cradle steer it by hand.

Nous aussi, nos treilles et nos ceps, et nous aussi nos carrières; parenté de production, parce que parenté de cœur et en tout genre.

Ici, où je me tiens, face à leur port, et à leurs carrières, je dis ces choses dans leur langue et presque avec l'accent qu'ils ont.

Langue d'oc, langue d'oc, tu restes fidèle à ce cours, et un chapelet de patois est le long de ce cours égrené, avec des grains de même bois, quoique de nuances un peu différentes, et ici est notre nuance.

Ici où la côte se dresse d'un coup, dans les vignes au-dessus de moi ils sont occupés à cueillir; ils pendent au-dessus de moi parmi les murs avec leurs hottes; et je tâche à cueillir aussi.

Ils penchent sous le poids des hottes en pleine hauteur du ciel, le mont debout dedans, et eux pendus au mont et moi au-dessous d'eux; et ici je me tiens dans ce Lavaux à moi, et près de ce Cully, ma ville, sous cette construction de pierre qu'est le mont, sous ces étages sculptés en murs, et je parle aussi cette langue pour des choses que je voudrais dire. Parlant ta langue ô Rhône, pour te dire, disant les hommes, disant les choses, disant les productions; et c'est à présent les hommes forts de chez nous, avec leurs moustaches humides.

Ils montent leurs escaliers: «Salut, ça va-t-il?» «Ça ne va pas trop mal et toi?» ils se parlent de mur à mur, d'en haut d'un mur d'en bas, ils portent le fumier sur leur dos, ils portent la

We, too, have our arbors and our vines, and also our quarries; there is a kinship of production here because there is a kinship of the heart in all things.

Here, where I hold on facing their harbor and their quarries, I say these things in their language and almost with their accent.

Langue d'oc, ancient language of the south, you remain loyal to this waterway, and a rosary of dialects extends and spreads along these currents like beads made of the same wood, although each with different nuances, and here is our own nuance.

Here where the coastline rises all at once, here in the vineyards above me they are busy picking grapes; they are suspended above me with their heavy baskets, among the walls; and I am trying to pick something too.

They bend under the weight of their baskets, their *hottes*, right in the middle of the sky, the steep hillside standing straight up within the sky, and all of them suspended from the mountain and me underneath them; and here I am holding on within my own place, the Lavaux, close to Cully, my city, beneath this construction of stone that is the mountain, under these shelves sculpted by stone walls, and I also speak this language in order to say the things I want to tell you. Speaking your language, ô Rhone, in order to say things about these men, these things, these productions; and at the moment I see those strong men from our country, with their damp mustaches.

They are climbing their steps: "Good day, how's it going?" "Not bad, and you?" They speak to one another from wall to wall, from the top of the wall to the wall below, they carry

terre sur leur dos; ils viennent, ils peignent avec un pinceau, et c'est tout leur pays qu'ils peignent, quand ils s'avancent entre les ceps avec le pulvérisateur: les feuilles et le bois, les échalas, les murs, eux-mêmes pour finir, faisant changer tout le pays et se faisant changer eux-mêmes.

Vignerons de chez nous, *vignerons* riverains du Rhône, qui est-ce qui vous envoie cette lumière à la figure, et il vous faut baisser les yeux? Qui est-ce qui vous envoie cette chaleur à la figure, et elle vous cuit la figure?

On a quand même de la chance: sans le lac, on ne serait rien, rien de rien. Où le Dézaley, ou l'Epesses, où le Calamin? C'est à l'eau qu'on doit le vin. Ça les fait rire.

C'est quand même à l'eau, voyez-vous, et est-ce vrai ou non qu'ils disent? alors ils se tournent vers les Savoyards.

N'est-ce pas que c'est vrai pour vous aussi, les Savoyards, et c'est pourquoi on vous fait signe; et eux: «Bien sûr, pour nous aussi.»

Alors c'est ça, on est amis. Encore une raison de l'être. Est-ce que vous ne viendrez pas une fois chez nous? on vous recevra bien, on a tout ce qu'il faut pour ça.

Et chante cette langue encore, dans cette causerie qu'on fait par-dessus l'eau, chante la chère langue à nous, la langue des pays du Rhône, qui chantera encore quand le Savoyard sera venu, et on lui dira: «Asseyez-vous.»

C'est qu'on a creusé dans le mont.

manure on their backs, they carry the earth on their backs; they come, the ones painting it all with a brush, and it's their entire country that they are painting when they move forward between the vine stocks and the spraying machine: the leaves and the wood, the stakes, the walls, making changes in the entire countryside and in themselves.

Winegrowers of our land, riverbank *vignerons* of the Rhone that showers such radiant light upon your faces, who makes you lower your eyes? Who sends this heat to your cheeks, burnishing your face?

Still, you are lucky: without the lake, you would be nothing, nothing from nothing. What would there be without Dézaley, or Épesses, or the Calamin? We owe a debt to the water for this wine. That makes them laugh.

Nevertheless, it's the water, you can see that, and is it true or false what they say? That's when they turn toward the Savoyards on the other side of the lake.

Isn't it true for you too, you Savoyards, and that's why they offer a gesture in your direction; and they reply: "Sure, for us too."

All right, there it is. They are friends. There's another reason for being so. Won't you come just once to the other side, to our place? You'll be well received. We have everything you need.

And this language sings again, this casual chatter above the water, it sings, this dear language of ours, the language of the land of the Rhone that will sing again when the Savoyard will have come and someone will say to him, "Have a seat."

And so they have hollowed out a place in the mountain.

25

Chez nous, ce qui se voit des maisons n'est pas tout, et le mont qu'on voit n'est pas tout: il y a encore ce qui est sous les maisons, il y a ce qui est sous terre: ces dix et douze vases, dix et douze mètres de tour, dix et douze mille litres l'un.

On vient, on s'assied; on ne s'assied pas toujours, on reste quelquefois debout; trois verres au guillon à l'un des vases, trois verres au suivant, et trois verres et encore trois, et lentement vidés parce qu'on ne boit pas pour boire.

On tient le petit verre, on élève le petit verre devant la flamme de la bougie, on regarde au travers; et c'est tout le pays qu'on voit, tout le pays qu'on boit ensuite, avec sa terre, son sucre, avec son odeur et sa sève, un goût comme quand on bat le briquet, et comme quand on a soufré et un goût aussi de sulfate; toutes les choses du pays et du sol, considérées, goûtées ensuite dans la substance de son vin.

Dans le verre se tient le ciel, se tient le climat, se tient le pays, on se tait devant le pays quand on l'élève dans le verre.

La belle saison dure ici (sous terre) toute l'année; ici on vient pour être au chaud; pas seulement le corps, le cœur qui est au chaud, dans ces cavernes de dessous terre, qu'on ouvre avec la grosse clef; et à la voûte ronde, tachée de moisi blanc, une grosse main noire va prendre le cigare, redescend avec le cigare.

In our world, what is seen from the houses is not everything, and the mountain that you see is not everything: there is still something beneath the houses, beneath the earth: these ten or twelve containers, ten or twelve meters of space, ten or twelve thousand liters in each.

They come and sit; but they don't always sit, they remain standing sometimes; three glasses at the spout of one of the big glass containers, three more glasses, and three glasses and then again three more, all emptied slowly because you don't drink for the sake of drinking.

They hold the little wine glasses and lift the glass up in front of the candlelight, looking through it; and it's the whole country that they see there, the whole country they are drinking then, with its earth and sweetness, with its odor and sap, a taste like the smell of a cigarette lighter just lit, like when it's time to add sulfates to the wine, also a taste like sulfates; everything of the land and the soil, everything is considered and then tasted in the substance of its wine.

The glass contains the sky, contains the climate, contains the land, so there is a silence to honor the land when they raise the glass.

Here, the beautiful season of wine lasts all year (below ground); they come here to be warm; not only the body, but the warmth of the heart, in the caverns under the earth that open with enormous keys; and into the round, vaulted cellar stained with white mold, a big black hand will take a cigar, descending again with the cigar.

Alors regarde, regarde encore, regarde tant que tu peux. Un bateau à vapeur fait une grosse fumée, le canot à rames est au milieu d'une espèce de tache d'huile.

Au milieu d'une tache d'un gris luisant est le tout petit canot noir, les peupliers a bord de l'eau penchent du côté droit par un effet de perspective.

Le lac monte devant vous comme la pente d'un pâturage, les perspectives des murs basculent, cette barque à voile est en haut d'un toit, cet autre toit pend dans rien du tout.

Ici est notre Méditerranée à nous; ici est une petite mer intérieure avant la grande.

D'en haut, et du point de cet arc qui est le point de sa courbure la plus marquée, les lieues vous sont offertes dans les trois dimensions; on peut dresser le mètre après l'avoir posé à plat, ce n'est pas la place qui manque.

L'immense ciel, qui se creuse au-dessus de vous, il se creuse aussi au-dessous de vous. Œil, trou percé, œil qui regarde et œil dans lequel on regarde, et on cherche dedans un regard en réponse au sien sans point en trouver dans sa profondeur.

Il semble qu'on voit l'autre côté de la terre et on va à travers la terre jusqu'au ciel qui est de l'autre côté.

Je viens aujourd'hui sous la pluie, comme je suis venu sous le soleil: ils ont changé toute couleur sous un ciel également tout changé, mais les mesures sont restées.

Par des chemins jetés en travers de la côte et qu'on suit, le cyprès vous est présenté. Les morts dorment sur le promon-

Look again then, and again, look as long as you can.

A steam boat is leaving a long trail of smoke, the row boat is in the middle of some kind of oil spill.

The very small black boat is in the middle of a gray, luminous patch of oil, and from this perspective, the poplars along the shore seem to lean forward from the right side of the lake.

The lake rises before you like the incline of pasture land, views shift from the stone walls, this sail boat floats above a rooftop, this other roof hangs there, in the middle of nowhere.

Here is our very own Mediterranean; here is a small, interior sea that comes before the big one.

From high up, and from the high point of this arc that is the peak of its sharpest angle, the vast distance beckons to you in three dimensions; you can lay the meter down flat then set it up straight, there's plenty of space.

The immense sky that caves in above you, it caves in below you as well. All-seeing Eye, a torn opening, eye that looks and eye into which you are looking, and you search within that gaze in response to your own without ever finding its depths.

It seems that you can see the other side of the earth and you cross over the earth to the sky on the other side.

I come today in the rain just as I came in the sunshine: they have changed colors beneath the sky that has changed completely too, but the proportions of one thing to another have remained commensurate.

On the coastal paths tossed sideways that I follow, you are confronted with cypress trees. The dead sleep out there on

29

toire. Ils sont couchés en dedans de cet éperon de terrain sous des croix de marbre ou sous des colonnes, sous de l'herbe, des rosiers sauvages, et, une fois qu'on a poussé la grille, on les voit comme dans ces chambres où la place manque et les lits ont été poussés l'un contre l'autre, si étroitement qu'on a pu. Le seul petit espace plat qu'on a trouvé leur a été réservé de façon qu'ils dorment ce nouveau sommeil honnêtement, couchés à plat dans le cercueil comme ils l'ont été dans leur lit. Et surplombent ensemble dans ce lieu le vide, faisant grappe au-dessus du trou. Les morts dorment ici sous les cyprès: c'est l'arbre. Dans l'angle de la cour, ces feuilles à trois doigts cachent la figue noire, ou l'autre espèce qui est verte, ou encore la blanche. Il y a déjà ces murs passés à la chaux et ces autres murs faits de galets ronds; les vraies maisons d'ici ont le toit coupé à ras la façade comme sont les tiennes, Provence d'ensuite, mais déjà annoncée ici. Les maisons de pêcheurs au bord de l'eau et quelques-unes de vignerons sous des treilles, avec la peinture bleue du sulfate qui a rejailli, ont toutes les mêmes tuiles en terre jaune, qui sont comme des moitiés de tuyaux. Ce pays n'a point d'arbres, ce pays est en pierre; rien que le pêcher de plein vent qui est un peu de brume rose, et puis un peu de brume grise. C'est ici un pays déjà d'architecture et seulement d'architecture, c'est-à-dire d'unité, non de diversité, un pays sans variété, un pays sans pluriel, imposant aux yeux son ensemble, et s'imposant aux yeux son ensemble, et s'imposant par son ensemble, non par son détail et par ses parties, prises isolément. Je vais comme je peux, et les images

the promontory. They are lying within this projection of land beneath marble crosses or beneath columns, below the grass, the wild roses, and once you push on the gate, you see them as if they are in rooms without enough space for beds and the beds are pushed against one another, as close as possible. The only small, flat space that could be found was reserved for them such that they sleep in this new, honest way, lying flat in the coffin as they did in their beds. And overlooking the emptiness together from this place, they form a kind of grape cluster above the gap in the rock. The dead sleep here beneath cypress trees: that is the tree. In the angle of the courtyard, these three-pronged leaves hide the black fig, or the other species that is green, or the white one, yet again. Already, there are these whitewashed walls and other walls made of smooth stones; the authentic old houses here have roofs cut short against the façade, like yours. You see them next in Provence but already they announce themselves here. The fishermen's houses on the shore and some of those belonging to the *vignerons* beneath grape arbors, painted with blue paint thinned by sulfate, all have the same ochre earthenware tiles, like half the drainpipes. This country has no trees, it's a country of stone; nothing but the fisherman under full sail who takes on the color of a pink fog, and then a gray fog. It's already a country with its own architecture, and only of architecture, which is to say of unity, not diversity, a country without variety, a land without plurality, imposing itself on your eyes all at once, and imposing itself on itself in its wholeness, not in details and parts taken in isolation. I am going along as I can, and the images

viennent; je laisse flotter au vent ces fils, sans penser encore à les renouer; ici, quand l'automne est venu, c'est comme un grand rayon de miel.

Voilà le soleil qui rebrille, et, posé tout contre l'eau bleue, seule la forme du rayon est affirmée, qui suinte mieux sa couleur dorée par cette présence de bleu couchée à plat dans sa proximité, ces jours d'automne où c'est encore bleu, et c'est bleu et doré, puis c'est bleu et roux. On se laisse tomber à un chemin qui descend droit en bas et qui est comme un lit de torrent entre ses deux digues. Par place, il y a des marches pour qu'on puisse s'y raccrocher. Les cailloux qu'on heurte du pied dégringolent longtemps devant vous: il semble qu'on va d'un bond atteindre ce fond d'eau, parce que quelques pas plus loin la pente tout à coup se dérobe, et il n'y a plus rien que le trou. Nudité, rien n'est là que la pente même et à nu, et, dessous, à nu, l'étendue. L'œil suit si loin qu'il veut le déroulement de ces rives et comment par endroit elles projettent brusquement tel promontoire pointu encore prolongé par un débarcadère, et puis tout là-bas le pays appuie la tête contre le coussin du Jura, mais c'est déjà un autre pays. Je tâche à montrer, n'est-ce pas? mon pays et puis un régime; alors je dis: ici, et je dis: pas là-bas. Je tâche à montrer une nature, une manière d'être, une manière de parler, une manière de bâtir, une manière de se tenir, une manière de marcher. Et je montre le roc, la vigne, le cyprès, le figuier, le pêcher; je dis ces murs, je dis ces toits, je dis l'architecture, l'architecture des maisons, l'architecture du terrain, je dis langue d'oc, hommes de chez nous, Valaisans,

come; I am letting these threads float in the wind without thinking too much about how to tie them together. Here, when autumn comes, it's like a great stream of honey.

There is the sun blazing again and, aimed completely against blue water, only the form of the sunbeam is affirmed, its golden color seeping through all the more because of this blue presence stretched out nearby, these autumn days where it is still blue, and it's blue and gold, then blue and rust. You allow yourself to tumble along a path that descends straight down like the bed of an onrushing stream between two dikes. In this place there are steps that you can hold onto. The stones that slip out from beneath your feet plummet for a long time before your eyes: it seems that you might reach the depth of the water in one leap because a few feet ahead the slope gives way completely, and there is nothing more after that but a hole of open space. Nudity, nothing there but the same slope and it is naked, and, below, it stretches out in its nakedness. The eye follows the distance, desiring the continuity of these riverbanks and sees how, in certain places, they suddenly jut forward as a sharp promontory prolonged, even more, by a dock, and then everything over there of the countryside rests its head against the cushion of the Jura, but that's already another country. I am trying to make it visible, is that clear? My country and then a regime; so I say: here, and I say: not there. I am trying to show a particular nature, a way of being, a way of speaking, a way of building, a way of holding on, a way of walking. And I point to a rock, the vines, the cypress, the fig trees and peach trees; I speak of these walls, these rooftops, I speak of architecture, the architecture of houses, the

Savoyards, Vaudois; et, cherchant à connaître enfin la cause de ces ressemblances, je vois l'eau, je trouve de l'eau, je trouve le Rhône et le lac; je vois les espaces du lac être pères de tout le reste, puis que ce lac est né d'ailleurs et que ce lac se porte ailleurs, que ce lac est un fleuve, que ce lac a un cours.

D'autres disent *Vater Rhein*, pourquoi pas nous aussi? dans notre langue à nous, par vénération et pour remercier, et affirmer une filiation et en même temps tourner le dos, parce que cet autre cours pousse vers le nord une eau verte, et celui dont il est question, c'est vers le midi une eau blanche ou bleue, et vers un plus grand bleu encore qui l'attend.

Les hommes d'aujourd'hui renient leurs familles de chair, et ils renient jusqu'à leur chair, ayant souffert à cause d'elle. Ils se cherchent des frères d'esprit par-dessus les frontières terrestres et des parentés autres que de naissance et de sang, ne se reconnaissant plus eux-mêmes dans ceux qui les entourent. Ils se veulent des frères d'idées et mettent leurs espoirs dans des parentés d'abstraction, parce que, disent-ils, nous sommes hommes avant tout, et le propre de l'homme est de discerner librement qui il est, de librement aller à qui lui ressemble. Ils se sont réfugiés dans les régions de la pensée par crainte et par dégoût de la réalité. Sur la terre, il y a, en ce moment-ci, trop de morts. La patrie, disent-ils, c'est où une même foi règne. La vraie patrie est la patrie des cœurs. Et leur patrie, ainsi, c'est une doctrine, leur patrie est un livre, leur patrie un enseignement; ils méconnaissent toute espèce de sol, et toute

architecture of cultivated land; I say *langue d'oc*, men from our homeland, Valasains, Savoyards, Vaudois; and in searching to know the cause of these resemblances, I see the water, I find the water, I find the Rhone and the lake; I find the vast space of the lake to be the father of all the rest, because this lake was born elsewhere and this lake carries itself elsewhere, because this lake is a river, because this lake has a flow of its own to pursue.

Others speak of "Father Rhine", why don't we speak like this too? In our own language, in veneration and gratitude, and to affirm a connection and, at the same time, to turn our backs, because that other current pushes its green water toward the north, and the one in question travels south, white or blue, and toward a greater blue that waits for its arrival.

Men today disown their flesh and blood families, and they deny their own flesh, having suffered because of their origins. They search for brothers in spirit beyond earthly boundaries and for relations other than those blood relations they found at birth, no longer recognizing themselves in those who surround them. They imagine themselves to be brothers in the world of ideas and place their hopes in a kinship of abstraction because, they say, we are men above all else and the particularity of man is to freely discern for himself who he is, to go freely toward those who resemble him. They have become refugees in regions of thought out of fear and out of disgust for reality. At this moment on earth there are too many dead. Homeland, they say, is where shared belief reigns. The true homeland is the homeland of the heart. And so their homeland is a doctrine, their homeland is a book, their homeland is a teaching; they misunderstand

espèce d'attache charnelle, comme si leur pensée tirait sa substance d'elle seule et se nourrissait de son propre fonds. Plus de nations, et plus de races: je viens au contraire noter ici la race, je viens dire le particulier et chanter le particulier; dire et noter une nature, telle nature, toute nature, dire et noter les différences.

Par amour quand même de la ressemblance, mais qui ne viendra que plus tard. Et l'amour du particulier, je l'entends pour l'amour de l'homme, et l'amour de l'homme particulier par amour de l'homme de partout (comme je tâcherai un jour de le prouver), mais d'abord j'ai à m'affermir à moi et aux choses autour de moi, à me connaître dans l'objet qui est le mien, parce qu'il est dans ma proximité; et je sens que l'objet lui-même me connaît mieux d'être dans ma proximité, à cause de ces fils tendus dès avant notre naissance de nous à ce qui nous entoure dans l'espace des races et le temps historique des destinées des races; oh! nous aussi couchés dans un berceau, nous aussi avec une nature et un pays penchés sur nous, un climat, tel ciel, telle lumière, telle nourriture, telle circulation de vents, telle direction préétablie, comme pour cette eau et ce fleuve, image de nous et de moi. Alors je me rassieds à ma parenté de famille, pour me rendre plus digne (un jour, si je peux) de mon autre parenté d'homme, mais pour l'instant, réinvoquant ces lieux, de nouveau ces villages sont nommés un à un, cette Savoie d'en face et les montagnes de Savoie,

every aspect of the soil that is their own motherland and every kind of attachment to their physical origins, as if their thought drew its substance out of itself alone and nourished itself out of its own depths. No more nations and no more distinctions among people. Here, to the contrary, I come to make note of the matter of races apart from the human race, I come to speak of particularity and to sing of particularity; to announce one nature as nature, all nature, to speak of this and point out the differences that exist among us.

Even as I sing out of love for resemblance, but that will only come later. And out of love for that particularity that I understand to be love for mankind and love for the individual man that comes out of love for men everywhere (as I will try to prove, one day), but first of all I have to strengthen myself and the things around me, to know inside myself the object that is mine because it is in proximity to myself; and I sense that the object itself knows me better for being in my proximity because of these threads that bind us together with all that surrounds us from before our birth in the world of our own kind and in the historic time of their destinies; oh! we too have lain in a cradle, with a nature and a country leaning against us, a climate, such a sky, such light, such food, such wind swirling around us, such a direction already established for us as for this water and this river, the image of us, and of me.

And so I return to the kinship of my family in order to make me more worthy (one day, if possible) of my other kinship with mankind but, for the moment, calling again on these places, once again these villages were named one by one, this Savoy

notre Lavaux, notre Jura, notre La-Côte; les villages de là-bas à noms de Saints et les nôtres aussi à noms de Saints: Saint-Gingolph, Meillerie, Évian, Saint-Paul, Thonon, Nernier, Yvoire; Nyon, Rolle, Saint-Prex, Morges, Lausanne, puis Cully, puis Saint-Saphorin, puis Vevey, Clarens, Villeneuve; tout ce cercle habité, cette circonférence d'hommes, ces petits toits partout mirés dans l'eau, ces villages entiers mirés, quand ils pendent dans le néant comme à un fil les jours de brume, ces taches jaunes, ces taches brunes, ces taches rouges; ceux d'autour du miroir nommés d'abord et désignés; et puis ceux d'en aval (et alors viennent les grandes villes, viennent Genève, puis Lyon); puis de nouveau des villages et des bourgs comme ceux d'ici, par une étrange ressemblance et une étrange symétrie, ces rochers roux du Villeneuve de là-bas (non plus le nôtre) et leurs ruines, Orange, Avignon, Arles, les vignes de là-bas (toujours ce torrent de montagne, toujours le galop du taureau), et enfin, près de l'embouchure, cette Crau qui répète les déserts rocheux de la source, parce que le vieillard revient à son enfance et il faut que le cercle soit complétement refermé.

O Méditerranée d'alors, n'est-ce pas qu'il convient que tu ressembles au berceau même?

Le berceau seulement plus petit, le tombeau plus grand.

Et même est-ce bien un tombeau? d'autres chantent l'âme de rien: on chante ici l'âme d'un fleuve, et cette âme ne meurt point. Voilà déjà qu'incessamment et chaque jour un peu nous reviens, ô Rhône, parce que chaque jour le soleil te dit: lève-toi, et t'attire à lui, par une vapeur qu'il fait monter de la mer,

across from us and the mountains of Savoy, our Lavaux, our Jura, our La-Côte; the villages over there named for Saints and ours too named for Saints: Saint-Gingolph, Meillerie, Évian, Saint-Paul, Thonon, Nernier, Yvoire; Nyon, Rolle, Saint-Prex, Morges, Lausanne, then Cully, then Saint-Saphorin, then Vevey, Clarens, Villeneuve; the entire inhabited circle, this circumference of men, these little rooftops mirrored in the water, entire villages mirrored there, suspended in nothingness as if by a thread of foggy days, these smears of yellow, these brown and red smudges; those named and established around the mirror; and then those downstream (and then come the great cities, then comes Geneva, then Lyon); then all of sudden the villages and towns like those here, with a strange resemblance and a strange symmetry, these ginger-brown rocks of Villeneuve from down there (no longer ours) and their ruins, Orange, Avignon, Arles, the vineyards over there (always this torrent from the mountains, always the gallop of the bull), and finally, near the mouth of it, this land called the Crau created by the confluence of rivers that repeats the rocky desert of its source, because the old man comes back to his childhood and the circle must be completely closed.

Ô Mediterranean. Isn't it right that even you resemble the cradle?

The cradle is only a little smaller, and the tomb greater.

Is it right to call it a tomb? Others might sing of an empty soul: one sings here of the soul of a river, and this soul never dies. Even now, you return ceaselessly, a little each day, ô Rhone,

et confiant cette vapeur au vent: « Porte-la d'où elle est venue. »
Nous aussi, nous saluons une âme, et au-dessus de ce cours, en
sens inverse, connaissons qu'il y a une autre espèce de cours.
Et des sagesses l'ayant suivi en même temps que les vapeurs,
des sagesses nous sont venues, des images nous sont venues,
des religions nous sont venues, en même temps que l'objet
Rhône nous revient et il nous revient chaque jour, comme s'il
s'agissait d'un corps, avec une circulation de sang, comme s'il
s'agissait d'un royaume, un royaume non politique, mais où il
y aurait tout de même un roi, c'est-à-dire un législateur, un en-
registreur des mœurs et des coutumes, une autorité qui décide
des actions, qui décide des paroles, qui décide des gestes.

O grande Méditerranée de là-bas, comme tu nous es étroi-
tement jointe, quand même tes bateaux ne nous arrivent pas
encore, mais il y a une autre navigation.

Voilà ici cette ébauche de toi, qui est faite parmi nos terres;
mais tu es du milieu des terres, Méditerranée, toi aussi.

Au milieu de nos terres petites, tu existes déjà en petit; que
je refasse alors briller nos eaux, pour que tu brilles mieux toi-
même.

J'ai connu ici tes orages, tes pâleurs, tes noircissements.

Souvent tes vagues m'ont empêché de dormir quand elles

because each day the sun tells you to wake up and draws you toward the light with a mist pulled from the sea by the sun's commanding rays, then confiding this mist to the wind as if to say: "Carry it forward from whence it came." We too, we greet a soul, and here above this current, in reverse, we know that there is another current flowing. And from the wisdom that has, at the same time, flowed from the mists, from wisdom we have come, from images we have come, from religions we have come, at the same time that the object that is the Rhone has come back to us and it comes back to us every day, as if it were a body with its own circulation of blood, as if it were a kingdom unto itself, a non-political realm, but where there would still have been a king, which is to say a ruler, someone keeping records of values and customs, an authority who directs action, who directs speech, who directs the gestures and movements of his people.

Ô great Mediterranean over there, like you we are closely joined, even if your boats no longer arrive on our shores, but there is another sort of navigation.

There it is, this sketch of you who was made here among our lands; but you are in the middle of all lands, Mediterranean, you too.

In the middle of our small lands, you exist already in a smaller form; and so, may I make our waters sparkle so that you, yourself, might sparkle all the more.

From here, I have known your storms, your pallor, your darkening.

Often your waves have hindered my sleep when they came,

venaient, trois et puis trois, et se tenant un court instant debout, ensuite se laissaient tomber de tout leur poids; ces nuits d'équinoxe où soufflaient ces cents qui viennent d'Afrique: alors les portes sont ébranlées, les fondations bougent sous terre, comme dans la gencive la racine de la dent.

Ces grands coups de pied sont donnés, ils ont avancé le bélier, ils balancent le bélier d'arrière en avant contre les murailles, ils attaquent le mont lui-même, le mont lui-même bouge, le mont lui-même est ébranlé.

Nuits où les vagues sont venues, nuits d'étoiles aussi, nuits de calme complet (ô diversité de ces eaux)! et est-ce qu'en toi aussi on voit, mer de là-bas, et dans tes eaux salées, les étoiles de nos eaux douces, si grosses, si rondes, si blanches, plus grosses et blanches que les vraies, quand une imperceptible ride les déforme et le quartier de lune monte et descend doucement comme le bouchon du pêcheur.

Nuits de vagues, nuits de calme; jours d'eau bleue, jours d'eau verte; jours de bise qu'elle est toute noire, toute noire et tachée de blanc à cause des moutons qu'il y a, comme on dit, c'est-à-dire ces crêtes défaites en écume; alors, le rivage d'ici est silencieux, les vagues sont pour les Savoyards.

Toutes les humeurs dans ce cœur, toutes les douceurs, toutes les colères. Sauvage, sauvage, ou si caressant, ça dépend des jours et du temps, si bleu des fois, si éclatant, et d'autres fois comme de l'ardoise; comme la fleur du trèfle, comme une joue de jeune fille, comme ces visages de vieillards cousus et recousus de rides et d'avance couleur de terre; blanc gris, couleur

three after three, and held themselves upright for a moment, then let go, crashing with all their weight; these nights of the vernal equinox when the winds that come from Africa: then doors shook and foundations rocked on the earth like the roots of teeth deep in the gums.

These great kicks were given ahead of the battering ram, they balance the battering ram from one end to the other against the walls, they attack the mountain itself, the mountain itself moves, the mountain itself is shaken.

Nights when the waves came, starry nights too, nights of utter calm (ô the diversity of these waters)! and there within you, distant sea, in your salt water, we see the stars of our own sweet water so full and bright, so white, more bright and white than the real ones, when an imperceptible ripple distorts them and the quarter moon rises and descends like a fisherman's float.

Nights of waves, calm nights; days of blue water, days of green water; days when the wind turns the water completely black, completely black spotted with white because of the sheep out there, as we say, which is to say the crests unraveling in foam; then, the riverbank over here is silent and the waves belong to the Savoyards.

With all the moods of the spirit of your heart, all the sweetness, all the anger. Wild, savage, or so caressing, which depends on the day and the weather, so blue at times, so sparkling, and other times the color of slate; like blossoming clover, like a young girl's cheek, like the faces of old men stitched and re-stitched with wrinkles the color of earth; white, gray, color of earth,

43

de terre, uni, taché, lisse, creusé, toutes les couleurs, toutes les allures; tous les silences aussi, toutes les espèces de silence et toutes les voix; quand il est comme l'amoureux qui chuchote des choses à l'oreille de sa bonne amie, quand il est comme l'écolier qui épèle sa leçon, quand il danse en chantant sur un rythme toujours le même, quand il brise au contraire le rythme, quand il se met à être rauque, quand il se remplit de tonnerres.

Je le peins encore une fois, je dis: «Voyez, la forme de ses rives est d'un berceau; sa forme intérieure est celle qu'il lui plaît d'avoir.»

Voilà que sa surface à présent se construit, parce qu'on la voit à distance et d'en haut; voyez qu'il est à lui seul un paysage.

A lui seul il est un pays et à lui seul une contrée, bien qu'enchâssé dans une autre contrée.

Il est enchâssé dans l'orbite, mais il existe pour lui-même, ayant sa construction à lui, ses pentes, ses coteaux, ses dépressions, son bombement, — qui monte tantôt, tantôt redescend, par un jeu de nuances.

Une barque qui vient encore: vous diriez qu'elle nous vient par-dessus ce grand monticule, ayant une côte à monter, puis une côte à descendre.

Grâce à ces dégradés, ces lumières, ces ombres, quand on regarde, par exemple, depuis la route de la Corniche, où un petit café rose pend sur le vide, et le cheval, attaché par la bride au tronc d'un platane, regarde vers en bas, et puis hennit, parce qu'il a peur.

unchanging, spotted, smooth, hollowed out, all the colors, all the allure; all the silences too, all kinds of silence and all the voices; as when a lover whispers in his girlfriend's ear or like a school boy who spells out his lesson, as when one who sings and dances always to the same rhythm breaks the rhythm and goes against it, as when the surface is rough and full of thunder.

I paint it, one more time saying: "Look, the shape of its riverbanks is like a cradle; its interior takes the form that it pleases."

That is how its surface takes shape at the moment, because you see it from a distance and from high up; look how it is a landscape unto itself alone.

Unto itself alone it is a land and unto itself alone a country, even if inserted in another country.

It is inserted in the orbit of another country, but it exists for itself, having its own construction, its slopes and hillsides, its hollows, its swells—that climb now then descend in a game of nuances.

A small boat reappears: you would think that it comes from this great rise, having a hill to climb then another to descend.

Thanks to these layers, these shafts of light, these shadows, when you look, for example, from the route de la Corniche along the ledge where a little pink café is suspended in the void and the horse attached to the trunk of a plane tree with its bridle looks downward, and then whinnies because he is afraid.

C'est d'ici que la bise, ayant longtemps attendu, couchée à plat ventre, se laisse tout à coup tomber, et le faîte des toits plie dans son milieu, comme l'échine de la bête quand le cavalier saute en selle.

Gare à ceux qui sont dans le golfe, s'ils ne connaissent pas les habitudes de l'endroit!

Là où un récif perce l'eau et où sévissent ces coups de bise qui ne sont annoncés par rien, des fois, se promenant dans des bateaux à voile, les ignorants ont été pris.

On réfléchit à toi de là-haut (encore) te considérant: tu es apparemment dans un état de subordination à tes rives: n'est-ce pas bien plutôt qu'elles te sont subordonnées? Tu es de partout dominé par elles et néanmoins tu les domines, dominé par elles matériellement, les dominant d'autre façon; dominateur que tu es, en effet, des cœurs, dominateur du souvenir, dominateur en tous genres d'images, subordonné par le relief terrestre, mais te subordonnant le relief intérieur.

Et puis même les choses subordonnées à toi, parce que tu es le grand calorifère, le grand régulateur, le grand réflecteur (et rappelez-vous, quand on demande à la grappe du Dézaley: «Qui t'a dorée?» ce qu'elle dit, et ces coteaux, rappelez-vous, si on leur demandait: «Où est votre soleil?» c'est vers l'eau qu'ils se tourneraient).

Parce qu'il y a deux soleils et le vrai est celui d'en bas.

Et les saisons qui ailleurs descendent du ciel, c'est ici des eaux qu'elles montent.

It is from here that the wind, after waiting a long time, sleeping flat on its belly, suddenly lets loose and the high point of the roof-tops folds toward the center like the spine of a beast when the horseman jumps up in the saddle.

Beware to those at sea, if they do not know the ways of this place!

Out there where a reef pierces the water and where gusts of wind strike without warning, ignorant ones out for a pleasant sail have sometimes been swept away.

One thinks of you from above (again), considering what you are: you seem to be in a state of subordination to your riverbanks: but isn't it more accurate to say that they are subordinate to you? They confront you in every direction, and nevertheless you dominate them, even though you are dominated by their materiality as you dominate them in other ways; predominant as you are, in effect, over hearts, predominant over memory, over all kinds of images, determined by the relief of earth, but here the rising land submits its interior shape to your authority.

And finally to the things determined by you, because you are the great oven, the great regulator, the great reflector (and remember, when anyone asks the grapes of Dézaley: "Who made you golden?" the reply is the same, for all these hillsides, remember that, if someone ever asked them: "Where is your sun?" they would turn toward the water).

Because there are two suns and the true one is the one down below.

As for the seasons that descend from the sky elsewhere, here they rise up from the water.

L'hiver se réchauffe à ces eaux qui fument; quand on y trempe la main, ces eaux sont tièdes pour la main.

Les petites poules d'eau qui plongent.

Sur la voie du chemin de fer noire et blanche, le corbeau prétentieux qui suit le rail en équilibriste, — et une mouette sur l'enrochement est immobile à côté du corbeau.

Elle semble écrire des choses sur l'eau avec son bec rouge parce qu'elle bouge un petit peu la tête de gauche à droite, tandis que cent autres dans l'air tissent et détissent sans fin comme les mailles d'un grand filet.

Des canards viennent. Les cygnes semblent des blocs de neige tombés à l'eau (parce qu'il y a un peu neigé).

Sur la voie du chemin de fer, le noir est le noir du charbon, le blanc est le blanc de la neige; une goutte seulement qui tombe de temps en temps dans la gouttière, et puis ces grincements plein l'air.

Et puis des gouttes aussi pendant aux fils du télégraphe, le long desquels elles semblent glisser comme des perles mal enfilées; et puis un autre grincement, c'est celui d'un bateau à rames.

Les canards se sont envolés les premiers, le corbeau se décide ensuite. Les petites poules d'eau se mettent à plonger et nager furieusement; des mouettes, quelques-unes semblent tout à fait rassurées.

Il y en a une qui est blessée.

Temps où il fait bon boire au chaud. Temps où il fait bon être à la cave; si on faisait les invitations.

Winter warms itself by these smoky waters; when you dip your hand in it, these waters are warm to the touch.

Little water birds dive into it.

Along black and white railway tracks is the pretentious crow who follows the rails like a tightrope walker—a gull sitting on the stone wall is immobilized by the crow.

The gull seems to write things on the water with her red beak because she moves her head a little from left to right while a hundred others in the air endlessly weave and unweave like the stitches of a great net.

Some ducks come along. The swans look like blocks of snow fallen in the water (because it is a little snowy).

Along the railway line, the black is coal black, the white is the white of snow; only a flake falling from time to time into the gutter, and then these grinding noises in the open air.

And then also some drops hanging from the telegraph wires where they seem to glide like poorly strung pearls; and then another grinding sound, this time the groan of a row boat.

The ducks took flight first, then the crow decides to go. The little water birds begin to dive and swim furiously; some gulls appear, some of them seem completely reassured.

One among them is wounded.

It's a good time to drink something warm. A good time to be in the wine cellar; if you have invited people to come. If you told all those who belong to us to come, even from faraway, because the trip is worth it.

Si on disait à tous ceux qui sont les nôtres de venir même de loin, parce que le voyage en vaut la peine.

A nos Valaisans d'en amont, à nos Savoyards d'en face, aux gens de Lausanne, aux gens de Genève.

Aux messieurs de Lyon même, et à ceux d'encore plus en aval, ceux de tout là-bas, ceux d'Orange, ceux d'Avignon.

Si on allait inviter jusqu'à ceux de Marseille, parce qu'ils reconnaîtraient vite quand même dans nos verres, et déjà rien qu'à sa couleur, le vin de Cassis qu'ils boivent chez eux.

Et reconnaîtraient le coteau sûrement, la côte sûrement, et reconnaîtraient cette eau sûrement, et tous reconnaîtraient les mots et leur allure, s'étant assis entre les grands vases et à la table qu'il y a.

Quand la bougie dans son bougeoir de fer battu une fois de plus, après avoir été éteinte, aurait été allumée (mais elle en a l'habitude), et de nouveau il y aurait les grandes ombres noires contre la voûte tachée de blanc.

Et il y aurait cette bonne tiédeur d'air, mais pas seulement cette tiédeur d'air, parce que les cœurs bientôt, eux aussi, seraient attiédis, et puis réchauffés, et les cœurs connaîtraient le rapprochement dans le vin.

Dans le vin, des choses sont dites, qui ne le sont pas à jeun.

Les natures se reconnaissent, parce qu'elles se laissent aller.

On va à la rencontre les uns des autres dans le vin: «Ah! ça m'a fait plaisir de vous entendre!»

To our Valaisans up river, to our Savoyards across the lake, to the people of Lausanne, to the people of Geneva.

Even to the gentlemen of Lyon, and to those even further downstream, those all the way down there, those of Orange, those of Avignon.

If you were going to invite people as far as those of Marseille, because even they would still quickly recognize, if only from the color, the Cassis that they drink at home when they see it in our glasses.

And would surely recognize the hillside and the shore, and would surely recognize this water, and everyone would recognize the appealing pace of the words, all being seated together at the table between large jugs of wine.

And when the candle that was extinguished in its forged iron candleholder, beaten one too many times, would be lit again (according to habit) there would be great black shadows against the vaulted ceiling stained with white.

And there would be this good warmth in the air, but not only this warmth of air, because hearts too would soon be warmed, and then reheated, and hearts would know that feeling of coming closer together in the wine.

In wine things are said that are not said on an empty stomach.

Natures recognize each other because they let themselves go.

You meet one another in the wine: "Ah! That gave me such pleasure to hear you!"

On n'ose pas dans la vie ordinaire. On a un mur autour de ses pensées. Il faut le vin pour qu'on saute par-dessus le mur.

Et on a un encore plus haut mur autour du cœur, qui ne peut pas s'abandonner, à cause des pudeurs qu'il a et non seulement à cause de ce qu'il a de mauvais, mais bien plutôt à cause de ce qu'il a de bon, et comme trop de respect envers lui-même; alors il est seul et cet autre cœur est seul; les cœurs sont côte à côte dans l'ignorance de ce qu'ils sont, sans conversation, sans échange, sans dons mutuels (de quoi ils peuvent pourtant seulement vivre), alors peu à peu ils meurent; heureusement que le vin est là; heureusement que nos caves sont là; faisons un jour la grande invitation, un jour qu'il fera mauvais temps, un jour qu'il fera du brouillard, quand la neige menace, quand on se souffle dans les doigts; tous nos parents, venez, on leur dirait, attention il y a trois marches.

Et alors trois verres de 19 pour commencer, trois de 17, trois de 14: «Ah! si c'est comme ça, je crois bien qu'on pourrait s'entendre.»

Et trois de 11, c'est le meilleur: «Comment dites-vous? Mais moi aussi!...» encore trois verres de 11.

«Dites-donc, vous n'avez pas faim? si on mangeait un morceau?»

«Femme (j'ouvre la porte), femme as-tu encore des noix fraîches?»

C'est quand la flamme de la bougie tremblote, éclairant mal, mais le cœur est éclairé.

One doesn't dare say a thing like that in ordinary life. You have a wall around your thoughts. You need wine in order to leap over the wall.

And you have an even higher wall around your heart that cannot abandon itself because of manners and modesty, and not only because of bad things, but even more because of the good, and out of too much self-respect; and so the heart is alone and the other heart is alone; hearts sit side by side in the ignorance of what they are, without conversation, without exchange, without shared gifts (without which, nevertheless, they cannot live), and so they die little by little; fortunately there is wine, fortunately our cellars are there; let's extend a great invitation someday, on a day of bad weather, on a foggy day when snow is threatening, when you breathe warmth on your fingers; to all our relatives you could say come, you could say this to them, but be careful there are three steps down to the cellar.

And then three glasses from 1919 to begin with, three from '17, three from '14: "Ah! if it's like this, I believe we would be able to understand each other."

And three from '11, that's the best: "What are you saying? But me too!..." again three glasses of 1911.

"Tell me, aren't you hungry? and if we had a bite to eat?"

"Say, woman (I am opening the door), woman do you have some fresh nuts?"

It is when the candle flame trembles in the waning light that the heart glows.

N'est-ce pas l'important que le cœur soit éclairé, que le cœur soit réchauffé?

N'est-ce pas l'important que les cœurs se réveillent et voient qu'ils vivent mieux, n'étant plus enfin qu'un seul cœur?

Parce qu'à présent on a été chercher les vieilles bouteilles et on s'assure d'abord prudemment dans le fond du verre qu'elles n'ont pas passé et qu'elles n'ont pas pris le goût de bouchon: «Rien du tout, mais c'est que c'est du bon, du tout bon…»

On trinquera pour l'amitié.

Nous aussi on est des bons, des tout bons, Pas vieillis, pas piqués. On trinquera pour l'amitié.

L'affaire est de se réchauffer, l'affaire est de se déboucher, l'affaire est de se retrouver.

Pas vieillis pas piqués, décantés seulement et parfaitement dépouillés; au contraire rien que le meilleur, le meilleur seulement qui reste, et alors: «Santé!» «Santé!»

Quand on trinquera à la ronde (quand est-ce que ce sera?) avec ceux de notre parenté, enfin connus de nous et enfin nous connaissant; et on boira à leur santé et à la santé du pays commun, on boira au lac et au Rhône, aux enfants du lac, aux enfants du Rhône…

(Si on faisait quand même cette invitation)…

Isn't it important that the heart be lit, that the heart be warmed?

Isn't it important that hearts awaken and see that they live better, being more, in the end, than one heart?

Because at present I've gone looking for old bottles and to be sure, cautiously at first, that they haven't gone bad down in the bottom of the glass, that they have not taken on the taste of cork: "Not at all, but it's good, absolutely good..."

We'll clink glasses together for friendship.

We too are good, all good. Not too old, nothing to sting or bite. We'll toast to friendship.

What matters is to warm up together, what matters is to uncork the bottles and find each other.

Not too old, not spoiled, only decanted and perfectly revealed; to the contrary, nothing but the best, only the best that remains; and then: "To your health!" "To your health!"

When we come together to raise our glasses in a circle (when will it be?) with our kith and kin, those ultimately known to us and those who know us; and when we drink to their health and to the health of our common land, then we'll drink to the lake and the Rhone, to the children of the lake, to the children of the Rhone...

(If, that is to say, we extended this invitation)...

Avec leur Pieta, avec leur Saint-Trophine, comment ils ont couché le corps du Christ percé de trous; comment ils ont sculpté dans la pierre, peint sur le bois, écrit sur le papier; au nom de cette parenté encore, au nom de toute parenté.

Celle de parler, celle de peindre, celle d'écrire; celle de bâtir, planter, se vêtir, prier Dieu, faire des lois, avoir des habitudes; celle des plaisirs, celle des amusements: les musiques, les instruments de musique, les danses, les espèces de danse, comment on se réunit pour danser, comment on fait la cour aux filles, les coutumes de chaque jour et les coutumes du dimanche, les habitudes de la table, les habitudes de l'auberge, les habitudes du travail à la maison et dans les champs, vendre, acheter, aimer, mourir; non seulement ce qu'on écrit sur le papier et dans la pierre, mais encore et surtout ce qu'on écrit d'abord avec des gestes dans l'espace, avec le mouvement de tout son corps dans l'air.

Et aussitôt cette écriture est défaite, l'air glisse autour de vous et déjà il ne vous connaît plus, le bras cesse de se mouvoir, l'espace a cédé à d'autres venues, les mots jetés ont fait leur bruit et puis se sont tus dans leur bruit; seulement d'autres autour de vous se sont déjà remis à écrire de façon pareille, la phrase interrompue est immédiatement reprise, le geste fait est refait, le mouvement est recommencé: alors durent quand même par continuité intérieure ces ressemblances de dehors.

O livre des parentés de sang, grand livre de la chair vivante, il faut te lire jusqu'au bout.

With their Pieta, with their St. Trophime, how they laid to rest the body of Christ, pierced with holes; see how they sculpted stone, painted wood, wrote on paper; once again in the name of this distant relation, in the name of all ancestors.

The ancestor who speaks, who paints, the one who writes; the one who builds, plants, clothes himself, prays to God, makes laws, holds to his own habits; the one with his pleasures and amusements: music, musical instruments, dances, different kinds of dance, how we come together for dancing, how we woo and court young girls, as a matter of every day custom and then with other customs on Sunday, our table manners, our habits of taking in guests, of working at home and in the fields to buy, to sell, to love, to die; it is not only what is written on paper and carved in stone, but also and especially what is written in the beginning with gestures in space, with the movement of the whole body in the air.

And as soon as this writing is unraveled the air glides around you and already it no longer knows who you are, the arm ceases to move, space has ceded to others who have come, the words tossed out have made noise and have then become silenced by their own noise; except that now the others around you have already started to write in a similar fashion, the interrupted line is immediately taken up again, the gesture you made is made again, the movement begins again: and so it is through this interior continuity that exterior resemblances endure.

Ô book of blood relations, great book of living flesh, it is necessary to read your pages to the end.

Je me suis laissé descendre à ce fleuve, comme on raconte que dans les anciens temps les morts lui étaient confiés; moi aussi, confié à son cours, porté par lui de phrase en phrase jusqu'à ce que la dernière fût venue, par quoi le livre prend seulement son sens, et seulement on touche à la totalité.

Celle où chante la langue d'oc, celle des vignes en étages; celle du roc perçant partout, la région des eaux rapides, ces régions du sud où les fleuves sont des torrents et se souviennent de la montagne jusqu'au terme de leur cours.

Langue d'oc des maisons, langue d'oc des cultures; langue d'oc des habillements, langue d'oc dans l'allure, langue d'oc dans l'accent.

Langue d'oc à muettes non muettes en oïl, langue d'oc de ce ciel et de la couleur de ces eaux; couleur d'oc du ciel et de l'eau, et transparence d'oc de l'air, langue d'oc du parler des monts, de la forme des rocs, des murs accrochés à la pente, de quand les hommes mettent de la terre entre ces murs, montant ensemble, de quand ils sulfatent, de quand ils ésherbent.

Et puis, sans le savoir, ayant accumulé lentement en eux cette substance, ayant recueilli goutte à goutte longuement au fond d'eux ce suc, ils ont eu besoin d'y faire goûter.

C'est en quoi ils se sont plus complètement exprimés: alors, m'exprimant à mon tour, je vais à cette expression d'eux pour mieux prendre conscience de la mienne.

I let myself come down to this river as one tells stories of ancient times when the dead were entrusted to it; I too, have been entrusted to its course, carried along by the river from sentence to sentence until the last one comes forth, which is the only point at which the book takes on its meaning, and only then achieves its unity.

One sentence singing in the *langue d'oc*, of the terraced vineyards; of rocks jutting out everywhere, the region of rapids, these regions in the south where the rivers become torrents and remember the mountains to the end of their course.

Langue d'oc of houses, *langue d'oc* of culture; *langue d'oc* in the ways of dress, *langue d'oc* in the pace of life, *langue d'oc* in the accented speech.

Langue d'oc of silences not silent in the northern tongue, the *langue d'oïl, langue d'oc* of sky and of the color of these waters; color of the south in the sky and water, and transparence of the south in the air, langue d'oc of speech in the hillsides, in the shape of rocks, of walls clinging to the slope when men pack earth between these walls, climbing up together, as they do when they spray the vines with copper sulfate or pull weeds.

And then, without knowing, having slowly accumulated this substance within themselves, having gathered the sap in their depths, drop by drop over a long time, they needed to share the taste of it.

They completely expressed themselves in it: then, expressing myself in turn, I turn to this expression of theirs to become more conscious of my own.

Ils ont assemblé des pierres, ils ont taillé dedans. Ils ont confectionné des panneaux de bois, ils ont peint dessus. Ils ont sculpté le bois. Ils ont pris la plume.

Ils ont fait prier des personnages dans la pierre comme eux-mêmes priaient, ils les ont fait pleurer et se réjouir, comme eux-mêmes pleuraient, se réjouissaient.

Il faut que l'édifice ait son couronnement, et tout en haut se tient l'expression désintéressée, ce qui n'a d'autre utilité que de faire sentir, faire connaître, faire aimer.

Ce qui ne sert à rien quand il s'agit de nourrir le corps, ou de le tenir au chaud; à rien quand il s'agit de devenir plus riche, à rien quant aux commodités, quant aux aises, quant au bien-être; nulles ressources matérielles, mais toutes les autres ressources, lorsque le jour vient qu'elles font besoin.

Les mots pour la beauté du mot, l'image pour la beauté de l'image, c'est-à-dire pour la joie qu'on tire de l'image; le Fils de Dieu mis devant nous en figure pour qu'il soit seulement plus vénéré.

Pour le prosternement des hommes, pour l'attendrissement des femmes, le signe de croix du simple passant; pour l'affirmation enfin de nous aux autres, l'affirmation d'une croyance, la proclamation d'une foi.

La proclamation de nous au total et de qui nous sommes, la proclamation d'une parenté.

Par le moyen de Ceux qui sont représentés, la représentation de nous, parmi ceux qui ne sont pas nous, en ce sens que nous

They assembled the stones carved from within. They made the wooden panels and painted them. They sculpted the wood. They took up the pen.

They made prayerful spirits inside these stones as they, themselves, prayed, they made the spirits weep and rejoice as they, themselves, wept and rejoiced.

The edifice must have its crowning glory and yet express indifference from on high, that which has no other use than to motivate us to feel, to know, to love.

That which serves no purpose when it is a question of nourishing our bodies, or of keeping us warm; means nothing when it is a question of becoming richer, or when it comes to commodities or comforts, as concerns well-being; no material resources, but all the other resources, when the day comes that these are needed.

Words for the beauty of words, image for the beauty of the image, which is to say for the joy that we derive from images; the Son of God placed there before us as a figure so that he alone might be cherished and more venerated.

So the men may bow down, and women might display their tender compassion, the simple sign of the cross of one who passes by the altar; finally for our affirmation to others, the affirmation of belief, the proclamation of faith.

The proclamation of all of us in the unity of who we are, the proclamation of kinship.

Through the means of those Saints represented, the repre-

sommes une région dans le monde, et une partie de ce monde, étant quelques-uns qui se tiennent ensemble grâce à une façon pareille d'aimer.

Une façon pareille de mettre certaines choses avant, certaines autres choses après: ainsi une construction et une hiérarchie de choses intervenue en nous, et préalablement aux constructions visibles, comme nos églises, nos châteaux, nos tours, la maison du bourgeois, la ferme du pays.

Et alors, moi aussi, tâcherai de coucher ce Corps percé de trous, parce que c'est un besoin, et même c'est le grand besoin.

Je ferai joindre les mains à mes Saints dans leurs niches, parce que c'est un besoin et même un grand besoin.

Je louerai ce qui est à louer avec des mots assemblés avec soin dans mon cœur, puis jetés sur le papier tout fumants encore de ce cœur, avec le plus de soin, le plus d'amour possible; et moi aussi, comme le peintre, de mon mieux, avec telles couleurs de mots et tels contours de phrases, figurerai l'objet de ma vénération.

Avec des mots sur du papier avec des couleurs sur de la toile, j'entends partout, j'entends de toutes les façons; et les pentes des montagnes ainsi se couvriront à nouveau de choses exprimées comme pour une seconde expression, les églises se peupleront de personnages parlant à nouveau pour elles, des livres seront lus, des musiques jouées; et toutes ces choses ensemble, milliers de choses peintes, bâties, sculptées, écrites, diront au cœur du monde qui je suis et nous sommes, qui sont tous ces hommes assemblés, – et que ce n'est pas par hasard

sentation of us that we are not us, in the sense that we are a region of the world, and a part of the world, being among those who hold together because of a similar way of loving.

A similar way of putting certain things first, and certain other things after: in this way we share a particularity, a construction and a hierarchy of things intervening within us prior to our visible constructions, like our churches, castles, towers, fine houses, like our farms in the country.

And then, I too, will attempt to lie down with the Body of Christ pierced with holes, because there is a need, and you might even say this is the great need.

I will bring my hands together before my Saints in their niches because there is a need and even a great need.

I will praise what is to be praised with the words carefully assembled in my heart, then tossed on papers still giving off smoke from the heat of this heart, with utmost care, with as much love as possible; and I too, like the painter, will do my best with such colors of words and such contours of sentences, I will depict the object of my veneration.

With words on paper, with colors on canvas, I hear sounds from everywhere, I hear them in every way; and in this way the slopes of the mountains will be covered anew with things expressed as if for a second time, the churches will be filled with people speaking for themselves once again, books will be read, music played; and all these things together, thousands of things painted, built, sculpted, written, will announce from the heart of the world who I am and who we are, who all of those assembled here are—and it is not by chance that they are assembled, but

qu'ils sont assemblés, mais qu'ayant d'abord été réunis par des occasions de nature, une expression commune les a ensuite réunis à nouveau, et si étroitement qu'ils ne sont plus qu'une seule personne.

having first of all been reunited by the vicissitudes of nature, a common expression has brought them together once again, and so closely together that they are no longer anything other than one single person.

C omme on verra peut-être encore mieux un jour, parce qu'il n'y a pas qu'hier, et il n'y a pas qu'aujourd'hui.

Qu'on dise encore la force que tu es, j'entends ta force matérielle; parce que tu es encore des centaines de milliers de chevaux-vapeur, des millions de chevaux-vapeur: Rhône industriel, Rhône des turbines, Rhône des usines, Rhône t'exprimant à nouveau par l'émission d'une énergie physique et cet Esprit physique en circulation dans des fils.

Voilà qu'émane dès à présent de toi une musique de machines à tisser et à battre le fer, et un chant de tisseurs et de batteurs de fer s'élève.

D'autres profondeurs d'eau vont être emprisonnées derrière des digues de béton; des chapelets de petits lacs artificiels, des écluses, des escaliers d'eau vont être patiemment au long de toi distribués; c'est ta vie matérielle qu'on te soutirera pour plus de vie parmi les hommes; mais de nouveau, quand même, une expression commune sera par elle portée au jour et je dis bien quand même une civilisation (une nouvelle espèce de civilisation).

Voilà maintenant les espaces ouverts à nouveau par toi, j'entends qu'on t'endigue, j'entends qu'on te drague, j'entends qu'on t'enchaîne et déchaîne, qu'on use, qu'on abuse de toi; on t'a plié à notre volonté, tu produiras l'esprit sur un signe de nous, mais l'esprit est toujours l'esprit quelle que soit sa nature opérante.

Quelle réunion plus grande concevoir qu'à présent que tu vas nous porter matériellement à la mer et non plus seulement

As we will one day, perhaps, understand better there is not only yesterday and not only today.

That we might speak again of the abiding force that you are, I turn my ear to your material force; because you still possess the strength of hundreds of thousands of horsepower, of millions of horsepower: industrial Rhone, Rhone of the turbines, Rhone of factories, Rhone expressing yourself once again through the emission of physical energy. And through the circulation of this physical Spirit flowing in your descendants.

From the beginning up to this moment this is what has come from you, a music of machinery for weaving and beating iron, and a song of weavers and forgers has risen up.

Other bodies of water will be imprisoned behind concrete barriers; strung in a succession of artificial lakes, locks, streams will be distributed like steps along your way; it is your material life that will be decanted to release more life among men; but once again, even so, a common expression will be carried along in it and brought to the light of day, and I mean to say a civilization will be brought to life (a new kind of civilization).

There are already new spaces brought out of you. I hear that they are holding you back, I hear that they are dredging you, I hear that they are chaining and unchaining, using and abusing you; they have bent you to our will and to produce your spirit under a sign from us, but the spirit is always the spirit regardless of the nature of the one who controls it.

What greater joining together can be conceived at this time than that you are going to carry us, materially, to the sea and no

y acheminer nos pensées? qu'on sera en bateau sur toi et les bateaux seront soufferts par toi; et que, par le moyen de toi la mer nous sera apportée.

La mer et ses produits et les produits d'au-delà de la mer, qui, ayant traversé la mer jusqu'à un port, par le moyen de toi traverseront ce port, se dirigeront vers les hautes terres.

On verra monter le bateau d'étage en étage, on verra le chaland grimper les escaliers; et là où la chute est utilisée pour le profit déjà des turbines en mouvement, cette même force de toi portera vers en haut, contrairement à tes desseins, les hommes vainqueurs et leurs marchandises.

Tu vas nous relier encore de cette façon-là au monde, et par une autre chrétienté, et plus qu'un poème de mots; — par ouverture directe et percement vers l'Océan, par une artère artificielle, mais branchée sur ce cœur des mers où va battre le pouls de l'Univers nouveau.

Parce que les hommes renaissent des guerres (et sont blancs ou noirs, jaunes ou rouges), mais partout regardent les uns vers les autres et se crient: «De quoi avez-vous besoin?»

«Je vous envoie ce qui vous fait besoin, envoyez-moi ce qui me fait besoin.»

Je vois qu'on va maintenant te plier à cette circulation-là, et on va te plier à cette espèce de communication-là; on va d'abord par toi satisfaire ces besoins-là et par toi fabriquer de quoi les satisfaire; mais les autres besoins naîtront néanmoins tôt ou tard, parce qu'ils sont les grands besoins.

longer be limited to transporting our thoughts in that direction, that we will ride your currents in boats and the boats will suffer from you; and that through you the sea will be brought to us?

The sea and its products and the products beyond the sea that, having crossed the sea to arrive at a port, will cross through that port, because of you, and will carry on, aiming for higher ground.

We will see the boats climb and rise, step by step, the barges clinging to the staircase of our land; and there where the waterfall is already used to set the turbines in motion for profit, this same force of yours will carry the conquerors and their merchandise higher still, contrary to your intentions.

In this way you will connect us to the world, and by way of another kind of Christianity, and more than a poem made of words;—by a direct opening that cuts through to the Ocean, by an artery that is artificial but that branches out into the heart of other seas where the pulse of the new Universe will be beating.

Because men emerging from their wars (and these are white, black, yellow, or red), look toward each other, and cry out to each other: "What do you need?"

"I am sending you what you need, send me what I need."

I see how they are going to bend you to this flow, and to this kind of communication; first they will use you to satisfy their needs and with your help manufacture what they need to be satisfied; but other needs will, nevertheless, sooner or later be born, because the needs are great.

Tôt au tard, nouveau un chant, tôt ou tard, de nouveau, une langue écrite, parlée et chantée, parce que c'est le grand besoin, et de nouveau une expression de toi, mais qu'il y ait d'abord cette base de vie nouvelle, cette forme nouvelle, et comme un sens nouveau à tout.

L'ouverture vers l'espace, la liberté dans l'utilisation, les trouvailles matérielles; de ces possibilités extérieures, les autres peu à peu naîtront; parce qu'il faut d'abord oser vivre, oser dans la vie, c'est-à-dire croire à la vie; et je ne vois derrière moi que des choses qui ont été osées, d'où l'action qu'elles ont encore sur nous.

On a prié là-bas d'une manière pour oser davantage, nous allons nous aussi prier, à notre manière à nous, mais pour oser nous aussi davantage; réconciliant par là le présent avec le passé, malgré les contradictions apparentes, et tous ceux qui vont se bouchant les yeux, ne voulant voir qu'une beauté et une espèce de beauté.

N'apercevant que les contradictions, non les ressemblances profondes.

Sooner or later, a new song will be heard, sooner or later, a written language, spoken and sung because the need is great, and once again this will be an expression of you, but first there is to be a foundation of a new life, this new form, and a new meaning to everything.

The opening toward a new space, the freedom to use it, material discoveries; from these external possibilities, others will be born little by little; because above all else you have to dare to live this life, which is to say to believe in life; and I see nothing behind me other than things that were dared, out of which those actions remain with us still today.

They prayed down there to be able to dare to do more, we will pray too, in our own way, daring ourselves to do more as well; as a means of reconciling the past and the present, despite the apparent contradictions, and despite all those who will cover their eyes, wanting only one kind of beauty and one space for beauty.

Seeing only the contradictions, not the profound resemblances.

E t puis cette autre continuité, quand même, parce qu'il y a qu'une vieille vie, quoiqu'il arrive, se continuera par-dessous.

Le soleil de Dieu luira sur nous et la terre de Dieu sous le soleil est cultivée.

Et sera cultivée. Avec les mêmes végétaux.

Avec les mêmes végétaux. Avec les mêmes espèces de cultures disposées de façon que chacune soit où elle doit, selon les convenances du climat et du lieu. Avec les mêmes sortes de blé, là où il vient bien, avec les mêmes plants de vigne, là où la vigne est à sa place. Avec les mêmes cultivateurs reprenant chaque année le cercle des saisons, parce qu'il y a des saisons pour eux, et ils sont des hommes de calendrier, penchés sous les Solstices, respectueux des signes du Zodiaque imprimés en rouge quand paraît le Bélier, et puis c'est le Taureau.

Eux qui se continuent et ne changent pas, parmi ce qui change, à cause qu'il y a toujours pour eux dans le ciel comme sur la terre les mêmes nécessités.

Ceux que j'aime, ceux de chez nous, ceux de la vigne revenus, ceux des coteaux où croît la vigne, et le premier printemps leur dit: « Plante les échalas », l'été leur dit: « Effeuille », et puis leur dit: « Sulfate », l'automne: « Récolte et pressure »; et l'hiver: « Maintenant va refaire tes murs. »

Et toute saison qui leur dit: « Travaille. » Et, comme les saisons reviennent régulièrement, ainsi ils travaillent régulièrement, n'ayant qu'à obéir.

And then there is this other continuity as well, whatever its source, which will continue from below because there is only one ancient life.

God's sun will shine on us and God's earth is cultivated under the sun.

And will be cultivated. With the same plants.

With the same plants. With the same species of crops arranged in such a way that each one exists where it must, according to the inclinations of climate and place. With the same kinds of wheat, there where it flourishes, with the same grapes clinging to the vine, there where the vines are at home. With the same farmers beginning once again the cycle of seasons, because there are seasons waiting for them and they live by the calendar, bending to the Solstices, respectful of the signs of the Zodiac printed in red when the Ram appears, and then the Bull.

Those who continue and do not change, living among things that change, because for them the same necessities are always there, in the sky as well as in the earth.

Those are the ones I love, those from our region, those who return like vines, those of the hillsides where the vineyards grow and where the first sign of spring speaks to them: "Drive the stakes" and where the summer says: "Pluck the leaves" and then tells them "Time to spray the sulfate" and in autumn "Harvest and press": and in winter: "Go now and repair your walls."

And every season tells them: "Work." And, just as the seasons return regularly, so do they work regularly, having no choice but to obey the command.

Ce lac peut-être ne sera bientôt plus pour d'autres qu'une espèce de grand réservoir de forces dont le cubage aura été jaugé, et le volume en sera maintenu par un jeu de vannes: empêchera-t-on pourtant qu'il ne projette vers où il faut la lumière qu'il faut et la chaleur qu'il faut?

Ils élèveront son niveau, s'ils veulent, ils feront monter son niveau jusqu'aux troncs des vieux saules creux, que les enfants remplissent de cailloux: entameront-ils en rien sa couleur?

Feront-ils que le vent ne se lève pas, que les vagues ne viennent pas, que le vieux vigneron, quand il veut, n'allume pas sa pipe de terre, du temps qu'il monte aux escaliers et s'arrête un petit moment pour souffler.

Là où sont seulement quelques éléments toujours pareils, les combinaisons sont simples.

Et alors plus haut combinez, combinez tant que vous voudrez: dessous demeure cette base de fidélité aux choses premières qui autorise par ailleurs tous les risques de la recherche.

Ce qui change, ce qui ne change pas, fusion et union et entr'aide, toutes les espèces d'utilité, pour toutes les espèces de beauté; rien n'est beau qui ne soit habité d'abord par la vie et la vie librement circule se créant sans cesse de nouveaux séjours et lieux de séjour.

Et quand même autour du berceau les deux anciens personnages se tiendront.

L'enfant qu'on aime vraiment, on l'aime pour ce qu'il est, non pour ce qu'on voudrait qu'il soit.

Perhaps this lake will soon be no more for others than a great reservoir of forces where the flow of water will have been measured, and the volume will be maintained by a game of waterworks: will they nevertheless prevent it from moving toward those place where its heat and light are needed?

They will raise the water level if they want, they will make it climb to the level of the trunks of old hollow willows that the children fill with stones: but will any of this bring about the least alteration in the color of the water?

Will they arrange things so that the wind no longer lifts off the water, or so the waves don't rise, or that the old *vigneron* will cease to light his earthenware pipe as he climbs the steps and stops for a moment to take a breath?

There, where a few elements are always the same, the combinations are simple.

And then the higher you go in search of combinations, combine as much as you like: down below rests a foundation loyal to essential things that, furthermore, authorizes all the risks of your search.

All that changes, and never changes, fusion and union and interdependence, every kind of utility, for all kinds of beauty; for nothing is beautiful that does not, first of all, dwell in life and in the free circulation of life, endlessly creating new destinations and dwelling places.

Even when our two ancestors hold fast to the cradle.

The child that one truly loves is loved for himself, not for the child one would like him to be.

Quoi qu'il arrive, l'amour demeure, cette base d'amour demeure.

L'homme continuera d'aller à la femme; la fille rit tournée vers le garçon.

Ils vont changer autour de nous jusqu'aux notions d'espace et aux notions de temps; qu'importe se vit toujours ce cœur qui fait de tout sa nourriture?

Voilà leurs fils et leurs tuyaux, leurs transformateurs, leurs barrages; une énorme conduite de fonte est maintenue fixée au flanc de la montagne à l'intention de quoi ils ont fait sauter le rocher: écoute quand même sous les pins trembloter la petite musique des orguettes.

Parce que c'est dimanche, alors ils sont montés. La fille se tient contre le garçon et le garçon joue des orguettes.

Six ou sept filles et autant de garçons, et ils tournent ensemble, comme avant, se tenant serrés, tandis que brille ce soleil jaune sur ce où c'est vert, et où c'est gris et où c'est rose.

Ces troncs de pins, le sol, de l'herbe, et il y a entre les branches ces morceaux de ciel comme des drapeaux.

Elle regarde quelquefois par-dessus son épaule et rit; puis, sérieuse de nouveau, s'applique seulement à bien régler sous sa jupe à gros plis le balancement de ses jambes.

Puis elle penche un peu de côté, ploie dans le milieu de son corps, se laisse aller, devient un poids; alors il faut qu'on la soutienne, mais il est doux de la soutenir.

Whatever happens, love remains, this fundamental love remains.

Man continues to go toward woman; the girl laughs, turned toward the boy.

Things will change around us, even our notions of time and space; but what does it matter if this heart lives on to make its own nourishment of everything around us?

There they are, their wires and their pipes, their transformer, their barriers; an enormous cast iron pipe is now fixed to the flanks of the mountain with the intention of blasting through the rock: listen, when even through the trembling pines you hear the gentle music of the organ grinders.

Because it is Sunday, and so they have climbed up there. The girl holds herself against the boy and the boy plays his music.

Six or seven girls and just as many boys turn together, as before, holding themselves close to each other while the sun pours its golden light on that place where everything is green, and then gray and then pink.

These trunks of pines, the soil, the grass, and there between the branches these fragments of sky waving like flags.

She looks over his shoulder sometimes, laughing; then, suddenly serious, applies herself only to carefully arranging things beneath her skirt of many folds in order to balance her legs.

Then she leans a little to one side, bowing down from the middle of her body then becoming a weight as she lets go. Someone has to support her, but it is sweet to support her.

Celle qui a les cheveux comme une grappe de raisins noirs et un peigne de cuivre est enfoncé dedans.

Quand il s'élève cette petite musique qui vient en tremblotant vers vous d'entre les pins, là-bas dans ce pays pierreux, où commence à luire en blancheur le fleuve, et on le voit fuir vers l'ouest.

Et plus loin vers l'ouest, au-dessus des montagnes, une lumière est dans le ciel; et alors tournez-vous vers le sud et devinez plus loin encore, au bas de cette autre vallée, par delà tant de lieues (mais l'esprit les contient sans peine) la lumière définitive qui règne sur la grande mer.

Elle a penché encore plus, donnant l'exemple, encore plus, et toujours plus, mais je saurai bien l'empêcher de tomber.

Je serrerai autour d'elle mes bras, qui ne dira plus non; je la coucherai à côté de moi, je lui tiendrai la main, elle se laissera faire.

Ils jouent encore leur petite musique; on entend l'explosion d'un coup de mine; toute chose premièrement est amour.

Rien ne naît que d'amour, et rien ne se fait que d'amour; seulement il faut tâcher de connaître toutes les espèces d'amours.

The one with hair like a bunch of black grapes and a copper comb buried deep within.

When this gentle music rises and comes toward you, trembling, between the pines, there in the stony countryside the river begins to glisten white and you see it fleeing toward the west.

And further on in the distance, above the mountains, you see a light in the sky; then turn toward the south and imagine even farther in the distance to the end of this other valley, and beyond it so many places (all contained by the spirit with no difficulty) where a definitive light reigns over the great sea.

She bends again, even more, making an example of herself, and then more, and always more but I will know very well how to keep her from falling.

I will wrap my arms tightly around her, she who will not say no; I will lay her down next to me, I will give her my hand, she will allow it.

They are still playing their gentle music; in the distance, you can hear explosives detonating; but everything is love before it is anything else.

Nothing is born without love, and nothing is made without love; only you must try to know all the different kinds of love.